Rhetoric in Postmodern America

REVISIONING RHETORIC
A Guilford Series
Karlyn Kohrs Campbell and Celeste Condit,
Series Editors

**Rhetoric in Postmodern America:
Conversations with Michael Calvin McGee**
Carol Corbin, *Editor*

**Analyzing Media: Communication Technologies
as Symbolic and Cognitive Systems**
James W. Chesebro and Dale W. Bertelsen

RHETORIC IN POSTMODERN AMERICA

Conversations
with Michael Calvin McGee

Edited by
CAROL CORBIN

THE GUILFORD PRESS
New York   London

©1998 The Guilford Press
A Division of Guilford Publications, Inc.
72 Spring Street, New York, NY 10012
www.guilford.com

All rights reserved

No part of this book may be reproduced, stored in a retrieval system, or transmitted, in any form or by any means, electronic, mechanical, photocopying, microfilming, recording, or otherwise, without written permission from the Publisher.

Printed in the United States of America

This book is printed on acid-free paper.

Last digit is print number: 9   8   7   6   5   4   3   2   1

Library of Congress Cataloging-in-Publication Data

Rhetoric in postmodern America : conversations with Michael
   Calvin McGee / edited by Carol Corbin.
      p.   cm. — (Revisioning rhetoric)
   Includes Fragments of winter : racial discontents in
America, 1992, by Michael Calvin McGee.
   Includes Bibliography of Michael Calvin McGee's works,
compiled by John Lucaites.
   Includes bibliographical references and index.
   ISBN 1-57230-278-X. — ISBN 1-57230-327-1 (pbk.)
   1. Public speaking.   I. Corbin, Carol.   II. McGee, Michael
Calvin.   Fragments of winter.   III. Series.
PN414.R438   1998
808.5'1—dc21   97-33135
                                               CIP

Permission to reprint the following material is gratefully acknowledged: Lyrics from "The Gambler," by Don Schlitz. ©1977 Sony/ATV Tunes LLC. All rights administered by Sony/ATV Music Publishing, 8 Music Square West, Nashville, TN 37203. All rights reserved. Lyrics from "Proud Mary," by John Fogerty. ©1968 by Jondora Music. All rights reserved. Lyrics from "Are You Sure Hank Done It This Way?" by Waylon Jennings. ©1975 Songs of Polygram International Inc. Used by permission. All rights reserved. Lyrics from "Smackwater Jack," words and music by Gerry Goffin and Carole King. ©1971 SCREEN GEMS—EMI MUSIC INC. All rights reserved. International copyright secured. Used by permission.

Preface

Collecting in print words that were spoken in dialogue succeeds only partially. This book began in conversations with Michael Calvin McGee, and it recognizes his belief in an embodied, living truth, even as his words appear here in disembodied print. This undertaking is as much to pay tribute to Michael as to remind us of his importance in the field of rhetoric. So it is fitting that several of his students should participate in bringing this book to life.

In the first chapter, John Louis Lucaites describes his introduction to Michael and situates Michael's theories and insights in the broader context of rhetoric. He also gives us a glimpse of the Michael McGee many of us have come to know personally—as a friend, tutor, mentor, and, for some of us, as the maestro. Chapters Two through Six reproduce Michael's conversations with me and Jan Norton during 1991. Chapter Seven is an essay Michael wrote using "performative criticism." In Chapter Two, Michael establishes the theoretical framework for the rest of his ideas by situating rhetoric (or the theory of power) in its relationship with science (truth or dialectic) and art (aesthetics or poetics). All discourse contains these three elements—aesthetics, truth, and power—for all discourse is embodied in some form, contains some coding of truth claims, and contains some coding of power. When we study rhetoric, we are studying power—theories of power, how one works one's will over others. Nevertheless, included in rhetorical study is consideration for the aesthetic form of the message (in the Althusserian sense) and the truth claims of that message (in the Foucauldian sense).

McGee works through the interaction of these three dynamics of discourse and the way they play out in representations and actions in the world. Through an understanding of the relationships of these elements, we begin to recognize the ideologies embodied in the representations. As we act out our lives in the real world where material conditions of our existence matter (and representations are integrated into our material conditions), we put into practice the kind of knowledge the Greeks would call *phronesis*—practical wisdom.

The *phronimos,* the person possessing practical wisdom, approaches history hermeneutically, rewinding and fast-forwarding the stories over and over again, looking for the subtle themes, subtexts, and threads that bind the history together in a coherent construction of a people or an ideology. We have a vast repertoire of representations through which to study the construction of ourselves, both as individuals and as a people. As rhetoricians, we study not only the great speeches that established political ideologies, we also study sitcoms and movies to seek those same themes, subtexts, and threads that tell us who we are.

In Chapter Three, "The Postmodern Condition," Michael adds Marshall McLuhan and Kenneth Burke to the mix to begin to understand how technologies have changed the way we do rhetoric. Orality, as our basic state, created a different kind of truth than the truth created in print. Oral truth leads to negotiated understanding; print truth leads to objective reality. The failure of the Enlightenment was in the fetishization of both print truth and objective reality. Regaining the place of negotiated understanding and practical wisdom is part of postmodern scholarly work.

Rhetoricians today face similar, though more complicated, challenges to what rhetoricians in premodern and modern societies faced. Rhetoricians help people deal with representations—the hyperreality of myths, legends, images, and Internet cultures—on a day-to-day basis through interpretation and critique.

But technology has had the effect of fragmenting cultures and texts creating this postmodern condition. This is both good and bad for rhetoricians; our jobs are not as straightforward. The postmodern condition requires us to work on the surface of our representations, piecing together fragments from the multiplicity of discourses, making sense of them, making arguments with them, and making judgments through them. We no longer, in the Enlightenment sense, seek a deeper truth or a deeper structure to repair. Now, rhetoricians must act as both audiences and speechmakers in their construction of coherent and believable texts—what Michael calls "performative criticism."

Chapter Four includes Michael's hopes for political change; his "hunt-and-peck" theorizing, which vacillates between conservatism and radicalism and ultimately winds up in rhetorical efficacy; and his belief in an ever-changing, ever-fragmenting society that requires rhetoricians to be as flexible as the culture they live in. The political Left needs to consider seriously Kenneth Burke's call to act rhetorically rather than politically correctly. There will be no Marxist revolution in the United States. We do not really want to overthrow the industrial state, according to Michael, because the consequences would be disasterous to the very people we most want to protect in a materialist sense. But free-market corporatism needs rethinking by the Left intelligentsia so that corporations are held accountable for the crimes they commit. This then brings into focus the relationships between law, morality, and liberty. For Michael, it is liberty expressed in terms of privacy—the individual's right to privacy and therefore the individual's right to an identity that, while different, "does not make a difference"—that is at the heart of American liberalism. American rhetoricians need to construct arguments for change in terms of liberty, rather than law, morality, or revolution, because "liberty" is the ideograph Americans embrace and defend.

Michael's concept of liberalism underlies his theories of "the people," "the public," "audiences," "spectators," and "the individual" in Chapter Five. In contravention to many Marxist and communitarian theories, Michael avers that the individual comprises the basic level of reality, not the group. Individuals construct their identities by the group affiliations they choose or have chosen for them. For Michael, ontology always precedes epistemology. Yet even as Michael theorizes the individual—tempering current theories of ideological control at the level of the body, thus reinforcing his belief in the preeminence of privacy—he also acknowledges the awesome power of the collectivity, of "the people." In the realm of politics, rhetoric acts to construct a believable "people" that individuals willingly embrace. Only through the feminized power of rhetoric will people act collectively, for coercion produces nothing more than submission.

The test of theory is practice—what Kenneth Burke calls "realism" and Michael calls "materialism." Michael's materialism (Chapter Six) is always grounded in "bread on the table and milk in the babies' mouths." Utopian thinking is beneficial only as far as it is practical, but that doesn't mean that rhetoric is ideal. On the contrary, Michael collapses the distinctions between language and action, or language and the material world, with instantiation of concepts and the dialogic process through which we recognize abstractions. Discourse is material; it acts in the world; it constrains; it punishes; it rewards. We can point to real-life instances of freedom, hope, or love as they are acted out among people. And our moral impulse arises from these instantiations. We are moved to stop the pain that we see in the world or in our homes, not because we abstract it from practice in order to theorize our response, but because morality is the core of our humanity.

In the final chapter, Michael presents his previously unpublished essay exhibiting his acting-out of rhetoric: "performative criticism." Here, as with most of Michael's scholarship, he puts into practice the theories in this book. Michael gleans pieces from the diverse discourses of Martin Luther King Jr., Spike Lee, Nike advertisements, and *Gabriel's Fire* to construct a text that addresses race and representational politics. As Michael says, "who we think we are, and who we want to be, are totems in the world of hyperreal simulations." As scholars, we deconstruct and reconstruct these totems, images, and representations as our moral impulse to stop the racism, to stop the pain. This is our most important application of rhetoric in postmodern America.

Contents

Part One

INTRODUCTION

Chapter One

McGee Unplugged

JOHN LOUIS LUCAITES
Indiana University

I first met Michael C. McGee in the fall of 1976 in Madison, Wisconsin.[1] I was a fledgling graduate student, struggling as hard as I could to demonstrate that I belonged in one of the premiere doctoral programs in rhetorical studies by trying to appear erudite and scholarly. McGee was a relatively new assistant professor recently out of the University of Iowa, seeking—with what in retrospect I believe must have been equal desperation and insecurities—to legitimize his presence and position of authority through the provocative strategy of appearing to be an intellectual outlaw. I don't mean by this to suggest any appearance–reality dichotomies here. What McGee taught and wrote was definitely in contrast with—and often hostile to—what at the time was the traditional approach to the issues and problematics of rhetorical studies; and, indeed, he clearly sought to open up new ways of thinking about rhetoric. But at least when I was first getting to know him in that first semester, the focus was on the appearance of radical intellectual and scholarly difference. Or at least that was my impression at the time. Only later would I learn that such *performances* were inherently rhetorical— the nodes at which appearance and reality articulated with and

3

fully engaged a particular audience's needs, interests, and desires.

McGee entered the classroom fashionably late that first day, after most of the students had arrived and taken their seats. Attired in blue jeans and flannel shirt, his hair tied back in a ponytail, his signature coffee cup in hand, he swaggered to the front of the room. He was accompanied, as if by marching bookends, by two similarly attired and hulking "good ole boys" (I was later to learn that they were also entering graduate students, whom McGee had mentored as master's students at Memphis State University) named Phil and Ben. One of them carried a hammer, which he laid down conspicuously on a table in the front of the room. I never asked why. They sat in the front row as McGee took his place behind a lectern, took a sip of his coffee, pushed his glasses back on the bridge of his nose with his index finger, raised his eyebrows, and without (further) fanfare began to describe the course—a series of lectures on the history of the philosophy of rhetoric from "then till now."

McGee's lecture that day (presented without notes, as was his practice) quickly moved beyond consideration of class requirements and procedures, and focused on what was to become a governing *topos* of the course: the rhetorical impulse. In McGee's vocabulary, the rhetorical impulse is an altogether natural, social motivation to employ language and symbols as the means of constituting and controlling one's social and political environment. The particular instantiation of the theme on that first day developed as a narrative about the omnipresence of rhetoric in the lives of "ordinary people": to an unemployed individual trying to discover how to account publicly for his economic failure, while saving just a patina of face and self in the process; to an aging and chronically arthritic woman, incapable of tying her own shoes or buttoning her blouse because of the excruciating pain in her hands, but nevertheless transfixed by the image of a televangelist who could persuade her to raise her hand in defiance of the pain and to declare her freedom; and so on. I had not previously thought of rhetoric in such quotidian terms. Nevertheless, as this professor and intellectual who oddly identified himself with plumbers in Paducah and southern, red-dirt tobacco farmers stood before me and described the significance of the rhetorical in the lives of such people, his characterizations resonated with my own blue-collar upbringing and took on a reality and significance that far exceeded my own prior and somewhat inconsistent assumptions about what rhetoric might be — namely, that it was monumental in the sense of great oratory, and yet that it functioned merely to mediate thought and reality. "Rhetoric" was being performed here as real and present in everyday life, as ontological, not simply epistemological; and for me, at least, McGee's performance of rhetoric's reality made it all the more compelling and likely.

For the remainder of the semester, McGee continued the performance, not just of being an intellectual outlaw — which admittedly had its own attractiveness — or of demonstrating the reality of the rhetorical impulse in everyday life, but also of enacting the ordinary significance of the age-old privileging of "philosophy" over "rhetoric" in Western culture. There was, of course, nothing per se new in engaging the philosophy–rhetoric debate. What was new concerned the ways in which McGee suggested that we treat every philosophy as a *rhetoric* designed to control some dimension of the human environment through the management of words and symbols, even as we treat every rhetoric as a *philosophy* that contains a theory of its own power to be successful. Conceived without the help of Antonio Gramsci or of Michel Foucault and the poststructuralists, all of whom McGee would only begin to study seriously once he returned to the University of Iowa as an associate professor in the early 1980s, he had put together a program of study that emphasized the (dis)continuities in the history of rhetorical theory and its almost constant engagements with philosophy and social theory.[2] At the same time, he also invited us to see the ways in which intellectuals — both "traditional" and "organic," although he didn't use those words — might weave such engagements together dialectically, in more or less provisional (though nevertheless always problematic) continuities as a means of understanding and addressing immediate social, political, and rhetorical problems. Rather than tracing the history of rhetoric from the pre-Socratics to Richard Weaver, Kenneth Burke, and Chaim Perelman in one magisterial swoop, as if reproducing the Great Chain of Being, McGee called attention to competing histories within our conception of the rhetorical—within the hands of both philosophical theorists and practitioners—and how they engaged and reacted to one another at various moments in time to account for, empower, and often control the rhetorical impulse. A great deal of attention has been devoted in recent years to rewriting the conventional history of rhetorical theory so as to undermine the mistaken and presumably natural continuities in the development of our understanding of its 2,500-year-old history, and, indeed, to situate the rhetorical as a uniquely cultural and ideological practice. McGee was there in 1976, not just arguing for such a program of study, but performing what today one might call an American poststructuralism. But more of that later.

As I got to know McGee better in the subsequent years of my socialization to rhetorical studies, I came to discover his commitment to the centrality of performance in the production and dissemination of knowledge and understanding, whether in formal lectures or published writings, or—for that matter, and perhaps far more important—in *conversation*. While I have learned (and continue to learn) a great deal from listening to, reading, and arguing with McGee's public lectures and published writings, it has always been in direct, oral conversation with him that I have profited the most. Frequently those conversations have taken place late at night in McGee's living room—a bottomless coffee pot brewing just feet away in the kitchen; Abigail, or one of his other cats, sitting on his lap or nearby; his personally programmed music playing on the tape deck in the background, both setting and monitoring the mood, sometimes bold and belligerent, sometimes soft and sultry, often with a touch of irony and mischief[3]; and the man himself, unplugged from the fetters of formal academic discourse, challenging whoever happened to be in the room at the time to perform as active adversaries and interlocutors, helping to probe and prod the rhetorical dynamics of the ideas, issues, and problems of the day.

The conversations that make up the bulk of this volume invite the reader to experience—and to engage—McGee unplugged. Of course, conversations are intrinsically oral and interactive, historically and socially specific. What we have here is a transcription, a written text of one side of an extended conversation that McGee had with two students, Carol Corbin and Jan Norton, in 1991. Unfortunately, no written text can replace what is thereby lost. Here, for example, among other things, the organization of these conversations into chapters (albeit unavoidable, given the conventions of scholarly publication) risks misdirecting the reader's attention away from the organic wholeness of an oral conversation and the ways in which an understanding of "formal discourse theory," "postmodernity," "American liberalism," "the people," and "materialism" might be implicated in and by one another in multiple and competing directions. In a real-time conversation with McGee, the movement from one topic to the next might be as dissonant as a shift from Roy Orbison to Public Enemy, or as subtle as a segue from Phil Collins to Nina Simone, but the separation of topics would never be as discrete or self-contained as titled book chapters. And, moreover, the conversation would never be static in the way that words on paper risk reifying ideas by tending to set their meaning in stone. Rather, conversations with McGee are always a dynamic critical performance, a jointly authored theorizing in the classical Greek sense of *theoria*—a looking at or viewing of a phenomenon as spectacle, always with an eye toward understanding and acting upon the world, *hic et nunc*. Indeed, one might conclude that such conversations with McGee are a rhetorician's direct challenge to Marx and Engels's eleventh thesis: Every act of interpretation is always already an attempt to change the world. Sometimes, however, McGee might add, the attempted change is not salutary.[4] By contextualizing McGee's voice as rhetorician, scholar, and pedagogue, one might begin to capture the sense and vitality, perhaps even the historical and social situatedness, of such an interaction; one might even hear and experience its orality and find oneself compelled to respond as a conversational partner. The thoughts that follow attempt to offer one interpretation of such a contextualization.

———————— ∾ ————————

But ol' Hank never woulda done it thissa way...
—WAYLON JENNINGS, "Are You Sure
Hank Done It This Way?"

Virtually since their inception in the early years of the twentieth century, American rhetorical studies have been plagued by feelings of academic and intellectual inferiority and an almost perpetual identity crisis. As a result, we rhetoricians have traditionally oscillated between borrowing our theoretical apparatus from other disciplines and resisting any complex or prolonged engagement with those disciplines as active partners in conversation on matters of common concern. The consequence, at least until the mid-1970s, was a kind of intellectual practice that restrained our ability to speak directly and effectively to the problems and possibilities of contemporary social and political life in anything more than mechanistic and unfeeling terms—what some have uncharitably characterized as "philosophy without tears."[5] The irony in this situation, of course, was that the classical roots of contemporary rhetorical studies had located rhetoric as a praxis precisely within the context of its promise to address the problems and possibilities of social and political life in pragmatic and effective ways. It was the perception of rhetoric's powerful influence and agency, after all, that led the Sophists, Aristotle, and early civic humanists like Isocrates and Cicero to valorize it, just as it led Plato and the philosophers who followed him to fear and vilify it. The clamor for politically and pragmatically vitalized rhetorical studies was beginning to be heard in the late 1960s and early 1970s, and we can witness its slow crystallization in the pages of the *Quarterly Journal of Speech* (*QJS*) during those years, as well as in volumes like *The Prospects of Rhetoric*.[6] But such talk was often eclectic and preliminary, as calls for disciplinary transformation often are, and it lacked clear and specific direction.

The mid-1970s saw several different efforts to address the centrality and significance of rhetoric to the contemporary world in more or less direct and sustained ways. The emergence of

McGee's voice as the lead essay in volume 61, no. 3, of *QJS* in 1975, "In Search of 'the People': A Rhetorical Alternative," marked one such effort.[7] On the surface, and at least initially, McGee's argument was quite simple: Rhetoricians had subtly argued themselves into the position of accepting and justifying the narrowly defined identity crafted for them by an academy—what he would later refer to ironically as the "knowledge industry"—governed largely by the twin values of objectivism and positivism.[8] The result was not only a stultifying reification of the problems of social and political change, manifested initially in McGee's controversial critique of the narrowness of vision of sociological, historical, and philosophical conceptions of "audience" and "movement," but a wholesale failure even to consider the significant role that rhetoric in practice might play in constituting such processes.[9] "In Search of 'the People' " thus functioned to demonstrate the necessary and inherent connections between rhetoric and social theory, between language-in-use and theoretical efforts to understand the processes of social and political change, particularly as they were empirically manifested *in situ* in the public usages of Anglo-American liberal democracy. This last point is most important, for the focus on the phrase "the people" was neither arbitrary nor serendipitous. Rather, it was guided by the quite conscious need to understand and critique the rhetorical source and dynamics of the voice of public and governmental authority in American social and political life—that is, the claim of popular sovereignty contained in and by the phrase "We the people."

"In Search of 'the People' " offered a provocative interpretation of the ways in which the phrase "the people" functioned in the Anglo-American context as a political myth that defined and warranted the social and political legitimacy of acts of power. The importance of that essay to rhetorical studies, however, exceeded the critical analysis of the centrality of "the people" to Anglo-American liberal democracy. Two dimensions of the essay in particular marked its disciplinary significance. First, McGee argued for a rhetorical conception of the problems of audience and effect that diverted attention away from studies of single speeches and/or sociologically defined social and political movements—the dominant mode of rhetorical critical analysis up to that time—and toward a study of culturally specific rhetorical practices and processes, especially the use of particular keywords and phrases such as "the people" that seemed to take on special significance in shaping and constituting public social and political consciousness. It would be several years still before McGee would name such usages "ideographs" and develop a complex understanding of the relationship between rhetoric and ideology as a theory of rhetorical movement, but even before he did that the implications were clear: Instead of our being forced into reducing rhetorical influence to simplistic and ultimately unprovable, immediate, cause–effect relationships, or being intimidated into ignoring the problems of audience and influence altogether, treating rhetoric solely in terms of its form or genre, we would be better served in our understanding of social and political change by focusing attention on the ways in which such usages as the myth of "the people" function in public documents as a process of defining and negotiating the life of the community. From this perspective, rhetoric is not simply a mechanistic or instrumental agency for social and political change, but an important hermeneutical source that provides more or less direct access to the very process of social and political change in action.

Of course, others in the mid-1960s had argued for attending to particular rhetorical practices and processes apart from the tradition of single-speech studies; Michael Osborn's work on archetypal metaphors and Edwin Black's work on form and genre come to mind as notable and important examples. However, none had done so organically, so as to emphasize a rhetorical conception of ideology, or in a way that explicitly placed rhetorical theory and criticism in direct dialogue with the main currents of thought in American and European social and political theory. That McGee did so marked the second important dimension of "In Search of 'the People'" for rhetorical studies. As he noted in the opening paragraph of that essay,

> Though concerned almost exclusively with public, social life, students of rhetoric have not been much involved with the

topics of social theory. I do not mean that we are ignorant and sloppy in our scholarship. . . . But as a rule, we tend not to recognize the significance of our own concepts in describing man's social condition. We bind ourselves to Greek and Roman understandings of rhetoric and thus tend to underplay our intellectual associations with such social philosophers as Voltaire, Hegel, Guizot, Burckhardt, Lamprecht, Marx, Dilthey, and Huizinga.[10]

The point was not to abandon Greek and Roman understandings of rhetoric, but to avoid treating them in a cultural and intellectual vacuum that restricted the capacity of rhetorical studies to engage contemporary social and political life in anything more than pedestrian and narrowly polarized ways. The rhetorical alternative McGee sought was to triangulate the terms and concepts of rhetorical theory (audience) with the problems and possibilities of social theory (mass consciousness and ideology) in and through a consideration of specific and situated rhetorical practices ("the people") as a means of generating a more complex understanding of the processes and functions of social and political change. His approach thus placed rhetoric, both as theory and as practice, in dialogue with social theory as a means of generating a critique of intellectual, social, and political practices that might enable a more progressive engagement with all three.

One might argue that virtually everything McGee has written since 1975 has been an attempt to explain, elaborate, extend, interpret, justify, correct, revise, or tease out the implications of "In Search of 'the People.'" To make such a claim, however, is *not* to argue that his program of writing and research has been static for over two decades, but rather to call attention to the complexity and multiple, overlapping dimensions that define its critical and theoretical scope. The search for rhetorical alternatives in both theory and practice has taken a number of twists and turns over the years, but remaining consistent throughout has been the unique effort to develop a critique of Anglo-American liberal-democratic practices that is at the same time the grounds for a critical reflection on the potential and possibilities of placing rhetorical theory in serious and sustained dialogue with contemporary social and political theory. It is in this regard that we might characterize McGee's program of study as an American poststructuralism.

Much of what we count as poststructuralist thought comes with a decidedly French accent—including most prominently the work of Jean Baudrillard, Gilles Deleuze and Félix Guattari, Jacques Derrida, Michel Foucault (especially in his "power/knowledge" stage), Jacques Lacan, and Julia Kristeva. This work underscores the materiality of the sign and the indeterminacy of meaning, and skeptically resists notions of an authorial subject or individual agency. To pair "poststructuralism" and "American," the latter with its strong connotations of realism, pragmatism, and individualism, might therefore seem oxymoronic. For McGee, however, paradoxes of this sort are not contradictory claims to be eliminated via the tenets of an *a priori* logic such as the law of noncontradiction, but oppositions or tensions—in the classical tradition, *stases*—that need to be managed and negotiated in the ways of rhetorical transformation and transcendence. And for McGee, of course, the key term for managing this particular tension is the word "rhetoric."

Rhetoric, McGee tells us, is a material phenomenon—the gestalt created in the particular context of a *speaker* addressing a *speech* to an *audience* on a given *occasion* with the intent of producing some kind of presumably affirmative *change* in the audience's beliefs, attitudes, and/or behaviors.[12] When speaker, speech, audience, occasion, and change coalesce at a historically particular moment in time, they create at least the potential for a force that can no more be ignored at the point of its impact than a bullet fired from a gun or an oncoming automobile can be. It has, in other words, a material presence rooted in the power of language to define and constitute social and political relationships. "Sticks and stones may break our bones," we teach our children, "but words can never hurt us." Of course, as adults we know better, and that is why we insist on teaching the aphorism as a way of softening the blow of hateful words. But as we all know, the imprint of such words can linger far longer and with greater effect on our sense of self than the physical scars of cuts and abrasions.

McGee's rhetorical materialism draws a connection with French poststructuralism in its recognition of the materiality of the sign. For McGee, however, who links postmodern conceptions of language-in-use with premodern or classical conceptions of rhetoric as social praxis, the indeterminacy of meaning and the "always-already-constructedness" of the subject in discourse are not angst-producing conditions. Rather, they manifest and invite the possibilities of human action and change. The absolute, autonomous individual may well be a fiction of the Enlightenment, but deconstructing the subject does not necessarily entail a complete loss of agency. An equally viable position extends from Marx's claim that "Men make their own history, but they do not make it just as they please, they do not make it under circumstances chosen by themselves, but under circumstances directly encountered, given, and transmitted from the past."[13] Of course, not all change is desirable, and so the progressive possibilities of subjectivity and agency, both individual and collective, always have to be read in and through the matrices of the rhetorical culture and sociopolitical context in which they occur—that is, what Marx refers to as the tradition or rhetorical history, which "weighs like a nightmare on the brain of the living."[14]

Rhetorical histories are always culturally specific. For McGee, the embodiment of the rhetorical history of American-style liberal democracy is simultaneously enabled and contained by the narratives, myths, metaphors, and ideographs that indeterminately constitute Anglo-American rhetorical culture. From this perspective, an American poststructuralism seeks to negotiate a dialogue between the philosophical deconstruction of social and political subjectivity, and the ways in which such subjectivity is interpreted and performed within the specific practices of American rhetorical culture. The point of such a practice is not to theor-

ize for the sake of theory, but to identify and exploit the pragmatic potential for rhetorical reconstruction. The critique that
emerges from such a dialogue works in at least two directions
at once—both qualifying our technical or academic understanding of the relationship between rhetoric and social theory, and
helping to transform our rhetorical praxis in progressive and
liberating ways.

You can't talk to a man with a shotgun in his hand . . .
You can't talk to a man when he don't want to understand . . .
                    —CAROLE KING, "Smackwater Jack"

Two important sites at which McGee has engaged the critical and transformative possibilities of a rhetoricized poststructuralism within the Anglo-American ideological context have been
the theoretical topics and rhetorical enactments of "power" and
"textuality." These are not the only such topics he has addressed,
but, taken together, his treatments of power and textuality help
to frame a dialectic in which one can begin to examine the significant potential that "a rhetorical alternative" poses for negotiating the exigencies of living in the contemporary world.

McGee is fond of quoting Salvo Hardin, the fictional psy-
chohistorian in Isaac Asimov's *Foundation* series, to the effect that
"violence is the last resort of the incompetent."[15] The social and
political truth of such a claim, of course, is in direct proportion
to the degree to which a world admits of rhetoric as a powerful
and compelling agency of action. In the absence of rhetoric as
an effective social praxis, raw physical force is all that one has
as a means of enacting one's will. In such a world, violence can
hardly be seen as a sign of incompetence. This is not to argue,
of course, that rhetoric is a complete replacement for violence
as a mode of action. Indeed, as McGee puts it in the conversations that follow, rhetoric is parasitic upon force; presumably,
we might conclude that in the total absence of the possibility for
physical violence, rhetoric would lose some of its edge as a desirable mode of social interaction. Or as McGee notes elsewhere,

"rhetoric is a species of coercion."[16] It gains a large measure of its effectivity from being a more desirable and comforting alternative to—perhaps sublimation of—physical force.

Nevertheless, the significant connection between rhetoric and power is not predicated simply on the opposition between persuasion and force—the carrot versus the stick—but on the capacity of agents to interpret and manage the *dynamics* or social energy in any particular historical context so as to direct and control individual and/or collective agency in socially and politically desirable directions. As McGee develops the point, that capacity is a function of the ways in which discourses are stylized in different rhetorical cultures and sociopolitical contexts. Power is thus not just the capacity to use force, but is an ideologically specific theoretical construct that is defined and functions differently in alternative rhetorical cultures. In the context of fascism, power is a positive point of identity—a function of *jouissance*, or the pure delight and desire in enacting the will for its own sake. Fascist rhetorics, as such, are stylized according to masculinized stereotypes of aggression. One wields power simply because one can, an arrogant and unfettered sign of individual or collective majesty: "*Ein Volk, ein Reich, ein Fuhrer!*" In the context of Anglo-American Whig liberalism, power is a negative point of identity, literally the opposite of "liberty"—that is, the feeling of *comfort* one gets in the presence of majesty and omnipotence. Liberal-democratic rhetorics are thus stylized according to feminized stereotypes of nurturance. Power is wielded legitimately only reluctantly and for a carefully considered greater good, the act of a loving parent disciplining a wayward child or an officer of state managing the tensions between "liberty" and "order": "Sweet is the name of liberty, the thing itself an object beyond all inestimable value."[17]

The rhetorical alternative to an understanding of power thus cautions us to think beyond the most direct and immediate effects of the use of force and coercion—an almost necessary condition in any collective arrangement where subjects are asked to subordinate their individual interests to the needs of a "greater good"—to the ways in which we collectively interpret and frame the *experience* of force and coercion. As such, it also encourages us to consider the implications of such usages, both positive and negative. This should not make us feel altogether comfortable in our usages of liberal rhetorics, for as McGee has pointed out on numerous occasions, there is a fine line of distinction between fascism and liberal democracy, particularly when placed within a nationalist context. What it should do is remind us of the need to attend vigilantly and critically to the ways and means by which we constitute our enactments of power, lest we risk succumbing to the dark side of the force of life-in-community.[18]

If you're gonna learn to play the game boy,
Ya' got to learn to play it right:
You got to know when to hold 'em,
Know when to fold 'em,
Know when to walk away,
Know when to run . . .
        — KENNY ROGERS, "The Gambler"

McGee's rhetorical alternative to power requires not only that we think of the use of force as it is rationalized and stylized in historically framed ideological practices, but also that we think more carefully about the ways in which styles of interaction are rhetorics. That is, style is not just the third canon of classical oratory, guiding the development of a persuasive discourse that moves from invention to delivery; rather style is quite literally the cultural frame that captures and contains — (con)figures — the range of possible meanings for a particular time and place. Others, of course, have recognized the need for more organic conceptions of style. McGee's point, however, is not just that style should be the master term for thinking of rhetorical practice, or even that style is fundamentally epistemological, but that the stylization of communicative interaction may well be the sum and substance of social and political interaction. Thus, for example, the emphasis in his earliest work was on the rhetorical styles of power and leadership.[19] This is a controversial point, to be sure, even for many rhetoricians, but it is one from which McGee has never swerved—from his first publication in *QJS* in 1970, "Thematic Reduplication in Christian Rhetoric," to the previously unpublished essay "Fragments of Winter" that concludes this volume.[20]

One entailment of this position is to call into question the rhetorical stability of textuality. An understanding of the rhetorical instability of the text has been there from the very beginning in McGee's work, although it has become increasingly pronounced (and more explicitly theorized) in recent years. It is important to note that McGee almost never privileges or features what we tend to think of as complete and discrete rhetorical texts in his analyses (i.e., orations, pamphlets, films, etc.). Such traces of the rhetorical process always appear, of course; however, it is not any one particular text that matters, but the ways in which clusters and fragments of such texts circulate within an economy of rhetorical usages that constitute a particular community. So, for example, his theory of the feminization of power does not emanate simply from the analysis of a particular speech or pronouncement by Queen Elizabeth, but proceeds by articulating the origins of Anglo-American conceptions of "liberty" within a larger narrative that incorporates a wide range of textual fragments—extending from the words of Peter Wentworth, Queen Elizabeth, John Knox, King James, Alexis de Tocqueville, and the book of Genesis to the words of Antun Robecick, a retired U.S. steelworker who ironically repatriated to his native Yugoslavia in the 1970s in search of "freedom."[21] Similarly, his construction and critique of "secular humanism" develops from a brief passage of Walter Benjamin's *Theses on History,* a fragmentary comment made by Jerry Falwell in a *Penthouse* magazine interview, and a series of readings of the book of Judges from *The Living Bible* (a version of the King James translation of the Old Testament).[22]

The significant text for McGee, then, is not simply the formal and final words of particular speakers, but the cultural text—the ideology—that is produced and performed in and through a larger, macrorhetorical process of active intertextualization.[23] In his earliest work he sought to excavate the cultural text of

Anglo-American liberal democracy as an overarching ideology with his focus on the rhetorical logics of ideographs. Ideographs are key ideological concepts such as "the people," "public trust," "liberty," and "equality," which serve as the consistent (because the signifier never changes) but flexible/unstable (because the signified is malleable and open to change) constitutive signs of American sociopolitical community.[24] They also typically mark the primary sites of battles for hegemony. Such discursive sites provide the canvas upon which rhetorical historians—whether as scholars writing in academic journals, or as public advocates speaking and writing to lay publics—frequently seek to bring the past to bear upon the present *and* to bring the present to bear upon the past, both with an eye toward (re)constituting the audience's collective future as a community. In more recent years, McGee's emphasis has shifted somewhat—though perhaps not as radically as many of his critics have suggested—from reconstituting the ideological tableau of Anglo-American liberal democracy as it *is* and *has been* to suggesting how we might yet go about rewriting the cultural text for our own times.

———————————————————— ❧ ————————————————————

Listen to the story now:
  Left a good job in the city,
  Workin' for the man ev'ry night and day,
  And I never lost one minute of sleepin',
  Worryin' 'bout the way things might have been,
  Big wheel keep on turnin',
  Proud Mary keep on burnin'...
        —IKE AND TINA TURNER, "Proud Mary"

This last point is important and bears emphasis. The disciplinary and political dimensions of the conversation McGee has featured in his work have not changed radically since their inception in the early to mid-1970s. Rather, his conclusion that rhetorical theory and American-style liberalism have failed to keep pace with potentially revolutionary changes in the patterns of social and political thought and practices have prompted him to cast the conversation in a different chord and key. According to

McGee, these changes, which he grudgingly admits constitute a postmodern condition, have been precipitated in part by major socioeconomic and demographic shifts that have occurred since World War II. Equally important have been significant variations in and usages of communication technologies that have accentuated the fragmentary nature of communal living. And in this postmodern condition, it is no longer enough for us as rhetoricians simply to enhance our understanding of the mere presence of rhetoric in everyday life, or to analyze the ways in which the instability of the texts in and through which we live are mystified as unitary and foundational.[25] We've made the rhetorical turn, with all that this entails—both for good and for ill. The genie has long been out of the bottle, and finally acknowledging the rhetorical turn does not change very much in the world if we do not learn how to live with it. Indeed, the great irony for McGee may well be that at the same time that we have acknowledged the rhetorical turn, we seem to have "forgotten to be rhetorical" (see Chapter Six, p. 156). The task before us as rhetoricians, then, is to (re)member the craft of rhetoric, to adjust our rhetorical practices to the demands of a radically changing world, and to develop strategies consistent with a postmodern rhetorical theory for managing and negotiating such change.

The history of rhetoric has always been a history of such adaptation and change. McGee suggests that this latest "new rhetoric" might do well to follow the path of performative criticism—an approach to critical theorizing modeled roughly on the classical example of Isocrates. For Isocrates, the rhetorician was a social surgeon whose task was to use rhetoric as a scalpel to craft and shape the moral resources of the body politic to produce a healthier and more productive organism *for the environment in which it resided.*[26] Of course, such theorizing is intrinsically rhetorical, not just in the sense that it focuses on the problem of rhetoric per se, but in the sense that it treats the production of theory—of knowledge and understanding in general—as a rhetorical process. To theorize in the postmodern condition is not to solve social and political problems once and for all, but to approach them as they exist in all of their contingency and par-

ticularity—to treat their material presence symbolically and crea-
tively, with and among one another as individuals-in-community.

To reframe this last point in terms of the metaphor that ani-
mates McGee's performances in this volume, a more productive
rhetorical theory for postmodern times may well require that we
remember how to converse, "the action of living or having one's
being in a place or among beings; the action of consisting or having dealings with others; living together; commerce, intercourse,
society, intimacy."[27] Such conversations, of course, demand conversation partners who are willing to be active and aggressive participants in the endeavor. The Enlightenment ideal of isolated, individual thinkers working out problems in private sanctuaries of
one sort or another no longer serves us well—if it ever did—in
dealing with the social and political problems of the contemporary world. Instead, we need a more dialogical model that invites
us to realize the ways in which our collective fate is tied up with
our ability to exist "within and beside oneself" as thinking and
doing beings that possess (or are possessed by) multiple and competing individual and collective identities.[28] To think of theory
as conversation, with its demands for particularity, locality, and
fluidity, might just be one such possibility worth considering.[29]

So pour yourself a cup of your favorite drink, turn on your
favorite music, and jump right in. The only rule is that you cannot be passive; you must engage the conversation actively, from
whatever social, political, economic, or intellectual sites define
your momentary place. It doesn't matter which "chapter" you begin with—or, for that matter, where in the "chapter" you begin—
for, like all good conversations, these conversations with McGee
double back upon one another in a variety of different ways, depending upon where you start and with what purpose in mind.
And if you are as lucky as I have been, they will repay multiple
engagements. *"And we're rollin', rollin', yeah, rollin' on the river . . ."*

NOTES

1. The middle name "Calvin" did not appear in print until 1980; its
   appearance coincided roughly with McGee's move from the Univer-

sity of Wisconsin back to his alma mater, the University of Iowa, in the fall of 1979. One better schooled in the ways of Freudian psychoanalysis might be inclined to make more of this than I do.

2. This is not to argue that McGee operated without a theoretical genealogy in this regard. In the early to mid-1970s, his work was rooted heavily in a conversation that he created among Edmund Burke, Kenneth Burke, and José Ortega y Gasset. As a graduate student, I often speculated that McGee thought of his writing projects as academic versions of a short-lived television program of the early 1960s, *The Meeting of the Minds*. This program was the brainchild of Steve Allen, who would script fictional roundtable discussions — conversations, really — among historical personages from different time periods, with an eye to how their interactions might generally resonate with contemporary problems and concerns. A typical script might bring Plato, Attila the Hun, Henry David Thoreau, and Catherine the Great together for a conversation.

3. In the late 1970s and early 1980s, McGee's musical repertoire consisted of an eclectic combination of rhythm and blues, Mississippi Delta blues, contemporary country and Western (especially that genre we might call "outlaw"), and '60s and '70s rock 'n' roll (including lots of the Beatles, Eric Clapton, and the Moody Blues). Carefully integrated with such sounds would always be the music introduced to him by his students and colleagues — everything from Canadian bluegrass bands to Pink Floyd. To appreciate the vitality and situatedness of these conversations with McGee, one has to hear them, in part at least, against the background of such music.

4. Marx and Engels's famous eleventh thesis on Feuerbach reads, "The philosophers have only interpreted the world, in various ways; the point is to change it." See "Theses on Feuerbach" in David McLellan, ed., *Karl Marx: Selected Writings* (New York: Oxford University Press, 1977), 158.

5. The quotation comes from Henry Johnstone's foreword to Richard A. Cherwitz, ed., *Rhetoric and Philosophy* (Hillsdale, NJ: Erlbaum, 1990), xvii.

6. Lloyd F. Bitzer and Edwin Black, eds., *The Prospects of Rhetoric: Report on the National Developmental Project* (Englewood Cliffs, NJ: Prentice-Hall, 1971).

7. Michael C. McGee, "In Search of 'the People': A Rhetorical Alternative," *Quarterly Journal of Speech* 61 (1975): 235–49.

8. Michael Calvin McGee and John R. Lyne, "What Are Nice Folks like You Doing in a Place like This?: Some Entailments of Treating Knowledge Claims Rhetorically," in John S. Nelson, Donald McCloskey, and Allan Megill, eds., *The Rhetoric of the Human Sciences:*

Language and Argument in Scholarship and Public Affairs (Madison: University of Wisconsin Press, 1987), 381–406.

9. The argument is developed further in a variety of places, but see especially Michael Calvin McGee, " 'Social Movement': Phenomenon or Meaning?", *Central States Speech Journal* 31 (1980): 233–44, and "Social Movement as Meaning," *Central States Speech Journal* 34 (1983): 74–76.

10. "In Search of 'the People,' " 235.

11. The lyrical fragment that belongs in this space is from the Eagles' "Hotel California." The particular fragment will be familiar to anyone who thinks of the Hotel California as an analogy for the perspective of "rhetoric." As many students who study rhetoric in our classes acknowledge: "Once I start thinking about the world in terms of rhetoric, I can never escape that perspective—no matter how much I try to leave it behind." The lyrical fragment, without this somewhat labored explanation, would have appeared in this space in a world in which "free speech" was truly "free." Unfortunately, Don Henley, who "owns" this lyric, refused to grant permission to reprint it because it has been receiving too much attention as of late. Fortunately, Don Henley does not own the idea to which the lyric is attached.

12. Michael Calvin McGee, "A Materialist's Conception of Rhetoric," in Raymie E. McKerrow, ed., *Explorations in Rhetoric: Studies in Honor of Douglas Ehninger* (Glenview, IL: Scott, Foresman, 1982), 28–31.

13. "The Eighteenth *Brumaire* of Louis Bonaparte," in *Karl Marx: Selected Writings*, 300.

14. Ibid., p. 398.

15. Isaac Asimov, *Foundation* (1951; New York: Bantam Books, 1991), 84.

16. "A Materialist's Conception of Rhetoric," 40.

17. Michael Calvin McGee, "The Origins of 'Liberty': A Feminization of Power," *Communication Monographs* 47 (1980): 23.

18. Michael Calvin McGee, "1984: Some Issues in the Rhetorical Study of Political Communication," in Keith Sanders, Lynda Lee Kaid, and Dan Nimmo, eds., *Political Communication Yearbook: 1984* (Carbondale: Southern Illinois University Press, 1985), 182.

19. See, e.g., Michael C. McGee, "The Rhetorical Process in Eighteenth Century England," in Walter R. Fisher, ed., *Rhetoric: A Tradition in Transition* (East Lansing: Michigan State University Press, 1974), 100–21; "The Fall of Wellington: A Case Study of the Relationship between Theory, Practice and Rhetoric in History," *Quarterly Journal of Speech* 63 (1977): 28–42; "Prerogative and Tyranny in the Nixon Years," *Exetasis* 4 (1977): 3–12; " 'Not Men, but Measures': The Ori-

gins and Import of an Ideological Principle," *Quarterly Journal of Speech* 64 (1978): 141–55.

20. See Michael C. McGee, "Thematic Reduplication in Christian Rhetoric," *Quarterly Journal of Speech* 56 (1970): 196–204. For a complete list of McGee's published writings, see the bibliography appended to this volume.

21. See "The Origins of 'Liberty'"; Michael Calvin McGee, "On Feminized Power" (The Van Zelst Lecture in Communication, Northwestern University School of Speech, Evanston, IL, 1985); and Allen Scult, Michael Calvin McGee, and Kenneth Kuntz, "Genesis and Power: An Analysis of the Biblical Story of Creation," *Quarterly Journal of Speech* 72 (1986): 113–31.

22. Michael Calvin McGee, "Secular Humanism: A Radical Reading of 'Culture Industry' Productions," *Critical Studies in Mass Communication* 1 (1984): 1–33.

23. See "A Materialist's Theory of Rhetoric," esp. 31–36.

24. Michael Calvin McGee, "The 'Ideograph': A Link between Rhetoric and Ideology," *Quarterly Journal of Speech* 66 (1980): 233–44.

25. Michael Calvin McGee, "Text, Context, and the Fragmentation of Contemporary Culture," *Western Journal of Speech Communication* 54 (1990): 274–89.

26. See Michael Calvin McGee, "The Moral Problem of *Argumentum per Argumentum*," in J. Robert Cox, ed., *Argument and Social Practice: Proceedings of the Fourth SCA/AFA Conference on Argumentation* (Annandale, VA: Speech Communication Association, 1985), 1–15.

27. *Merriam Webster's Collegiate Dictionary,* 10th ed. (1994), s.v. conversation.

28. McGee derives the phrase "within and beside oneself" from the tension between *alteración* ("being besides oneself") and *ensimismamiento* ("within-oneself-ness") in José Ortega y Gasset's *Man and People,* trans. Willard R. Trassk (1957; New York: Norton, 1963), esp. 11–37.

29. McGee's most recent project to advance the possibilities for such rhetorical conversation went on-line in the fall of 1996 with his home page (http://www.uiowa.edu/~commstud/Fragments/) dedicated to critical rhetorical theory. The title of the home page is "Fragments." The opening screen introduces itself to its readers as follows: "Welcome! This is a scholar's page dedicated to discussion of critical rhetoric and ideology in the postmodern condition; to distribution of electronic versions of scholarly essays on rhetoric; and to Net resources for rhetorical study. Most resources here point left to the posts: postmodern, poststructural, postmarx, postcolonial, postCalvin and Hobbes. You'll also find an emphasis on 1,001 uses

of dead Greeks, because antiquity and postmodernity have more to do with one another than either with modernity." Here one finds, among many other things, an effort at collaborative writing that invites any and all conversation partners to contribute to an on-line hypertext essay on "ideology," as well as to make contributions to a glossary of terms relevant to the problems of critical rhetoric.

Part Two

THE CONVERSATIONS

Chapter Two

Formal Discursive Theories

In Western civilization there are three master terms for thinking about discourse: "beauty," "truth," and "power." There is a complete theory of discourse that is argued through the lens or through the agency of each of those terms: beauty, truth, and power. Beauty has to do with pleasure, with aesthetics. To create a theory of discourse for thinking through aesthetics, we talk about that dimension all the time; it is poetic. Truth, then, is seen through the lens of philosophy, and power through the lens of rhetoric. One reason why the ancient Greek theories of discourse — poetics, dialectic, and rhetoric — survive and seem to speak to us to this day is that they were organized around these three master terms through which it is possible to think about all of life.

"Rhetoric" is that theory of discourse which was created, or would be created if we didn't know about it, in consequence of thinking about the relationship between discourse and power. "Poetic theory" or "aesthetic theory" is a theory of discourse that was created to think about the relationships between discourse and beauty. And "science" or "philosophy" or "logic" or "rationality" is the theory of discourse that was created to think about the relationship between truth and discourse.

The difficulty, of course, arises because there is no single discourse. No discourse is only truth-seeking, only beautiful, or only powerful. This is the most important lesson that Kenneth Burke taught us—the lesson of perspective taking, of horizons that need to be viewed. These terms are lenses, dimensions, or facets of discourse. These characteristics of discourse are all present to a degree in any discourse.

There is nothing that cannot be represented in discourse. We can create something discursive to imitate, mimic, parallel, or represent anything else. So, in that sense, everything always already has a discursive dimension to it. We achieve a great advantage when we think about things as discourse. What we have to keep in mind is that a good theory of discourse will not get a rocket ship to Jupiter. A good theory of discourse will not flatten a mountain, build a dam, make a city, or feed the homeless. Mathematics won't do it either. Mathematics is a powerless form of discourse, because mathematics is empty representation. "Two plus two equals four" is a very sensible statement. The difficulty is that it's so abstract it says absolutely nothing. It means to be thoroughly empty of content, because two of anything plus two of anything equals four of anything. As long as we don't know what it is two of and two of and four of, we have a statement that is not about reality.

What makes the Enlightenment sort of a villain in history is that since the Enlightenment we have fooled ourselves into believing that there are only two dimensions in our world—that we live in a tension between beauty and truth. And we try to ignore power. We pretend that power is something that either will go away if we ignore it or will be undermined by truth or beauty in the end.

I was once very interested in aesthetics and very much a devotee of Nietzsche. Once in my life, I actually read everything that had been translated that he wrote. But the Vietnam War happened, and as I frequently say to people, I got my aesthetes shot off in the war. I lost a lot of my empathy for aesthetic views of the world. For a period of about fifteen years, in a very formative time in my life, I simply ended the conversation with literary people, because in my mind literature was not concerned with anything except fads and fashions. I still refuse to acknowledge the artistic status of James Joyce, for instance. The difficulty is that I just don't understand why something I can't read, can't understand, and don't like gets called great art and great literature. Something I read, understand, and like very much is called either old-fashioned, a classic, or pulp nonsense. I don't understand how the reality of power can be—as it was until very recently—so systematically ignored in literary circles. I would concede that in the last twenty years or so there are scholars on the literary side who have given some attention to power. But I notice that among the very scholars who give it such attention, the one casualty is literature itself.

Communication studies were ghettoized by people in literature for a long period of time, and it was virtually impossible for us to carry on a conversation about what we studied, simply because it was immediately trivialized. Since the days of Carlyle and his insane polemics against threshing machines, literary people have been inveterately opposed to technology, particularly technology in regard to entertainment or things that are roughly literary. Films came in; literary people didn't study films because they were vulgar, they were popular, they were the movies. Then people began to study them for a while, found they had an artistic flair—and then it became "film art" and it was okay to study it. And the same is true with television today.

RHETORIC

I was having real trouble with my master's thesis, trying to conceptualize something. A visiting professor from Berkeley, Todd Willey, came to Cornell, and he sounded great to me. And he sat down and talked with me for about an hour, and I tried out some problems on him. And he listened for about thirty minutes or so and he said, "Michael, I think I know what your problems are. First of all, you need to understand that rhetoric has to do with words. You study words when you study rhetoric. These philosophies and social theories that you're talking about are all fine, but think about them through words. The second problem that you have, it seems to me," he said, "is that we study bad literature. You're holding up all these people and yourself to account for all the deficiencies that these people say exist, and trying to show how they don't exist. You have to understand that as far as those people are concerned, neither you nor your object of study exists." And I opened my eyes, and he told me a little parable about being at Berkeley and getting into a conversation with an English professor. He figured out finally that the guy didn't really know what he was studying under the heading of rhetoric. So the English professor said, "What's rhetoric?", and Willey responded to him with this: "Rhetoric is lies and bullshit. Every department in this university is devoted to the search for truth, except us. We search out lies and bullshit. Now I put it to you, which are there more of?"

Of course, since every discourse has an aesthetic dimension as well as a power dimension, we must consider the relationship between aesthetics and power. Althusser is extremely interested in this. He wants to understand the connection between ideological critique or ideological analysis and art more than he wants to understand the connection between ideological critique and science or truth. Althusser's theories, like the theories of Mao Tse-tung, suggest that ideology constitutes a curriculum and not a process. For Althusser, it is a curriculum that can be reformed. Althusser's participation in the '68 crisis, for example, suggests that the entire curriculum of a university can be reformed. A university can be created that is a Marxist university. They did it, and if they can do *that*, why can't a new ideological curriculum be created through practice and criticism and replacement? But the question is, what should replace the old curriculum? And here's where Althusser loses me. He replaces it with Stalinism. He's an apologist for Stalinism. He modifies it and corrects it, but he doesn't want to give up Stalin as part of the root in history.

In this move toward aesthetics is the suggestion that once we discover the correct ideology — in Althusser's case, Marxist–Leninist ideology — what really matters is not so much the ideology itself or the curriculum itself, but the way in which it is taught. How do we go about teaching it? How do we get people to internalize it in themselves? And that's his interest in art and aesthetics.

Linking ideology and art is the right thing to do, and Althusser's description of the Ideological State Apparatus and its relationship to the Repressive State Apparatus is crisp and clear and uncontroversial. But I don't want to read Althusser as saying anything much more complicated than that sometimes movies can be about politics. Spike Lee's movie *Do the Right Thing,* for example, forces the connection between ideological analysis and art. We can't talk about racism in America without talking about ideology. An artist can choose to do a political subject; Spike Lee's *Do the Right Thing* or Picasso's *Guernica* are good examples. When that happens, the art invites ideological analysis. It participates in and invites an analysis of the text's power coding.

Another example is the television sitcom *Cheers.* I can do a rhetorical critique of it in which I will expose what I believe to be the power relations that are coded and embedded in the discourse. I can take the same show and describe how personal relationships are worked out, so that an aesthetic of love or an aesthetic of interpersonal relationships is what that text is about. We have John Fiske on one side who suggests that this text— *Cheers*—can *only* be read as coded for power. And we have my former student Mary Piccirillo on the other side saying, "No, because I can read this text as coded for beauty."

As a theory of power, rhetoric talks about how opposing ideas and opposing people relate to one another in discourse and how people create discourse in the context of which to execute their power plays and power moves. Rhetoric shows us how to argue, which is a way of defending ourselves against attack. It shows us how to justify. It shows us what counts as evidence, how to find evidence, how to do research. It shows us how to approach judgment. And it also tells us how to make judgments and how to justify our judgments. In other words, it shows us how to write the majority and minority opinions in a courtroom situation. And it shows us how to justify our judgment once it is made. It is purely a technology of power.

Virtually nothing about rhetoric is innocent of this power. Pick any rhetorical principle, and we'll put it on the table, and I'll show you how it's connected with power. Whether we talk in Aristotelian terms of rhetoric as persuasion, or more contemporary Burkean terms of rhetoric as identification, both of these concepts have to do with using our *will* in order to make an outcome come true. It is *in* and *through* and *as* discourse. We are attempting to control our environment in particular ways by promoting an identification with other people or by persuading other people.

If we are in the business of identification, we're into community building. Every person we add to our community makes us more powerful. What's really interesting is that so many people are afraid of this notion, because they're afraid of the whole notion of power to start with. The minute we start talking about power, we get very fearful responses. People will innocently say they're not concerned with power, but every time they succeed in building community, they increase their power. Community building is a power play.

Fundamentally, there's no difference at all between domination and empowerment. Power is power is power. When we say that we use power the right way, or we use it the wrong way, what we're saying is that we're drawing the line between empowerment and domination. Or, more precisely, what we're saying is "From my perspective, it's empowerment." And someone else is saying, "From my perspective, it's domination." We're making an angle judgment. Or we're making a moral judgment. But fundamentally, in terms of the mechanics and techniques, it's exactly the same.

Although Foucault says that power and knowledge are collapsed because he wants to emphasize that knowledge is power, there is a distinction between power and knowledge. Knowledge is not devoid of its power elements, certainly. And all discourse that pretends to be philosophy or even mathematics actually has an element of rhetoric in it. There's rhetoric in everything. There's power in all discourse. Power and knowledge are interpenetrated. But Foucault never really considered the opposite point of view. He never looked at the discourse of power to discover how the penetration worked the other way. We need to consider knowledge aspects in power discourse as well.

Rhetoricians in this country particularly have made a fault out of studying the discourse of power. If you look at most rhetorical critics or theorists in the 1950s, they were studying Presidents and Congresspeople and Senators—all people with positions of power. They weren't studying the margins of society at all until after the 1970s. We've done nothing but study producers of power and the degree to which the discourse of power is penetrated by knowledge. And our conclusion has been—not much.

We know that politicians are going to lie. We know the way they're going to lie. We know the particular devices they're going to use, the circumstances in which they're going to use them, and the ends that they hope to achieve. The claim that there is dissimulation going on in rhetoric—that there is lying going on, concealing of motives—is an indication that knowledge is present but is being specifically coded out of the discourse in order to maximize its power.

Knowledge can and must find its way into discourses of power, based on the circumstances. As we move from a relatively primitive democracy into an advanced industrial or postindustrial state, things get so complicated that power can't be exercised without knowledge. There is no way that a politician can develop an energy policy without knowing something about the differences between nuclear power and coal-generated power, and what the relative risks of both are. Policy makers depend on experts to provide this information in most cases. But politicians have to know what they're talking about, and knowing what they're talking about becomes one of the indications of their character, their conduct; and voters judge when they choose them. When we study discourses for power, we have to think about both power and knowledge as coding devices. And that's the way to carry Foucault's point further.

For example, a college professor can be both a political candidate and a college professor at the same time, but the discourse sounds different when this person is wearing the two different hats. When out in the political arena, the college professor is going to downplay the fact that he or she is an intellectual and an egghead, and he or she is going to do an awful lot of "just plain folks" talk. In the academy, just the opposite is going to go on. The professor will say, "I'm not just plain folks. I didn't fall off the turnip truck yesterday. I have my PhD from Yale, and I've studied this problem for a long time." These two different strategies in self-presentation are really coding systems. One is being coded for power in order to avoid offending the majority of people and to attract the majority of people as voters. The other is being coded for knowledge, in order to claim exceptionability — not a commonality with other people, but the possession of exceptional knowledge.

Foucault is suggesting that we're dealing with a correlative relationship between power and knowledge. Certainly there's an element of power in a classroom. There's no question about it. But it is more reductionist to characterize that as a relationship of power than to characterize the politician's discourse as discourse of knowledge, because so much is being done in the classroom to counteract and counterbalance the possibilities of power relationships. Every student from the sixth grade on recognizes the coding system that tells when a teacher is on a power trip. We know when a teacher is being too harsh in his or her discipline. We know when a teacher is unsure of himself or herself. And all of the codes that indicate, "I know what I'm talking about," "I care about you," "I'm here to teach you," are in place. And yes, power is there; there's no question about it. But it is reductionist to reduce the situation to power alone, just as it would be reductionist to reduce the PhD politician to knowledge alone.

Knowledge and truth are informed through dialectic, but rhetoric is informed through hermeneutics. Dialectic assumes that we can get at the truth of something — that we can eliminate contradictions, that we can eliminate the distance between a representation and the thing that is represented. Hermeneutics is interpretation. It is knowledge that is not either true or false, but simply negotiated. Negotiated knowledge is what derives out of rhetoric. Why do we negotiate except as an instance of power? The key word here is "interpretation," and I think the key question is "What constitutes knowledge?" or "What is truth?" If we are willing to say that truth is an interpretation—the best interpretation that we can make at this time, given our knowledge—then we're involved in hermeneutics. In a Platonic dialectic, on the other hand, we are not going to be satisfied with a simple interpretation. We want the truth. We want to approach the world of forms. There's an inconsistency here, because most of the people involved in philosophical hermeneutics are great devotees of dialectic. But their version of dialectics is far more conversational than Plato's was.

Every interpretation necessarily anticipates action. There's no reason for us to come to any conclusion at all about what something means—what this history means, for example—unless we intend to act. There's no reason for us to know immediately. We can suspend judgment, keep studying, keep reflecting, and keep thinking. The only time we are satisfied with an interpretation is when there's a necessity to act upon it. So every interpretation necessarily anticipates rhetoric—unless we just simply persuade for the sake of persuading and pass around the ignorance, which is what Plato said about rhetoricians. Every rhetoric anticipates taking some kind of action. The rhetorician has invested an awful lot of labor in terms of properly interpreting what one is to act on, and how one is supposed to behave. So every rhetoric presupposes a hermeneutic.

In Marxism and in Marxist literary criticism in particular, when two things are opposite and inconsistent, it's called a "contradiction." And logic demands that we eliminate the contradiction. But in rhetoric when two things are opposite and inconsistent, we don't call it a contradiction; we call it a *stasis*. And we say that at that moment, judgment is required to make a choice. We don't eliminate the contradiction, we manage it. We make a judgment so that things come out best. Marxists are trying to find contradictions and resolve them. But that's why this kind of thinking belongs in rhetoric and not someplace else. Rhetoric is the theory of discourse or the theory of society that depends on managing contradictions rather than dismissing them.

It's easiest to understand the difference between rhetoric and dialectic in a court of law. There are a certain number of arguments that you can make that Jones is innocent. And all the arguments that could have been made about the innocence of Jones, believe me, have been made. We've tried Jones six ways from Sunday for the last 400 years. So it's a question, if you're an attorney, as to which argument you're going to make. And there are standard topics that attorneys look for: Was there a motive? Was there opportunity? And so forth. And the attorney constructs a theory of the crime on the basis of responses to this relatively tight series of *topoi*. It's all a narrative construct that lies behind our understanding of every one of the criminal accusations.

The same is true with ideology. The truth of all these things is purely rhetorical. We don't assume that this is *the* answer, that this is *the* motive that Jones had. We simply assume that when we put what we know about this case in the proper construction, it is a reasonable explanation. We also know that the prosecution is going to say something diametrically opposed to this. And we *assume*, if we're rhetoricians, that we're going to be opposed — *not* that we have the truth, but that we're going to be *opposed*. And that there's going to be a third party and a fourth party, a jury and a judge, and they're going to be free not only to choose between the constructions but to make adjustments for things we've left out of our story. The judge can instruct the jury to ignore one part of the story. The jury can come back in and say, "You didn't consider this, and because you didn't consider it, you didn't prove it. And we're going to find the defendant not guilty." So they're all subject to a thing called "judgment" that is part and parcel of rhetorical criticism.

DIALECTIC

The models of rhetoric and dialectic are identical, except that in dialectic there is an assumption that a clash of views will yield an increase in knowledge for both people. When you become aware of what your conversant opponent said, and make your conversant opponent aware of what you believe, the result is a net increase in knowledge for both of you that is greater than what you came in with. This is called a "synthesis." A dialectical clash of opinions produces greater knowledge—synthesis. And therefore dialectic is associated with knowledge.

There are a number of important dialectics, and the model of thesis, antithesis, and synthesis can, at some level of understanding, be used to represent any one or all of them together. The first dialectic is Plato's, and it is one of question and answer, where the function of the questioner is to reveal error or ignorance in the person who has claimed something. So if someone says, "I saw a purple Martian last night," rather than responding, "You did *not* see a purple Martian last night," I would say, "Well, is that right? Where did you see this? When did it happen?" I'm searching for confirmation and for ways to correct. This is based on Plato's commitment to a kind of fundamental realism, in which he suggests that the language that we use to describe the world and act in the world is not transparent.

The second important dialectic comes from Aristotle, who did with Plato's dialectic very much what he did with every other body of learning. He was a quantifier and systematizer. Probably the most important book of the *Organon* or the Aristotelian logic is *Topica* or *Topics*, and here Aristotle lays down the rules of dialectical disputation—how dialectic is supposed to operate, how the conversation is supposed to go.

Kant, who revised dialectic, organized his philosophy in terms of the bifurcation. His books, as they were published originally, had two columns. One was titled "Said pro" and the other "Said contra," and he was simply arguing *for* something in the left-hand column and then *against* it in the right-hand column. Then he thought about those arguments on both sides of the question. What he said pro, he said contra; what he said contra, he said pro. And then the page itself would come together in a normal printed one-column page called the "synthesis," where he would make a judgment between these two positions and add a little bit to it and come to the "truth" that he had arrived at.

Hegel was different from Kant primarily in his belief in the fundamental reality of dialectical reasoning. Kant was just working on a method of reasoning, a way to think through problems. But Hegel wanted to take the position that not only was this *a* way of reasoning; this was *the* way of reasoning, the one that revealed the mind of God. Hegel was motivated through his entire philosophical career by trying to understand the mind of God. He believed that the mind of God was revealed in the rational order of the world, and he believed that the dialectical logic, as he thought Plato and others had practiced it, and as Kant had perfected it, actually mirrored nature. The dialectic was the form of things in nature. So nature was formed dialectically. Everything was in a set of oppositions: male and female, plant and animal, and so on. Since nature was organized dialectically in a system of oppositions, then clearly the mind of God must be dialectical also. In order to demonstrate this, he studied the natural history of ideas and wrote his famous histories in which he showed all of the ideas evolving out of the competition of forces historically.

Then we have Marx's dialectic, and Marx was a young Hegelian to start with. But Marx's dialectic differed from Hegel's in the sense that he stopped looking for God. He suggested that one of the problems of Hegel's philosophy was that all of the oppositions that he was seeing between good and evil, and so on, were always already programmed into his philosophical project by the fact that he was searching for God. He had a Christian agenda, and Marx believed that we didn't want our ideas to descend from heaven, out of the scriptures. He wanted to be rigidly empirical. Marx became a philosophical materialist. Because of this, he looked at ordinary conversations of real people and looked at the conflicts that were developing there through history. And what he found there was not a competition between good and evil, and right and wrong, and good conscience and morals. What he found was a fight for bread on the table and milk in the children's mouths. Marx materialized Hegel's idealistic dialectic.

The way in which I have distinguished between the model for rhetoric and the model for dialectic in associating rhetoric with power and dialectic with *episteme* is part and parcel of classical rhetoric. It is what Plato and Aristotle had in mind all along. The Greeks *did* say it all; it's just a matter of deciding what they meant. Aristotle said that rhetoric is the counterpart of dialectic. "Counterpart" is a dramatic or dramatistic term. "Part" and "counterpart" have to do with the staging of a Greek play. The main actors are on stage, and behind them is a Greek chorus that will make commentary on the action directed at the audience. The real representation is going on among the actors on the stage, and the Greek chorus is a counterpart. It's part of the harmony. Therefore, rhetoric is metadialectic. Rhetoric is dependent on dialectic; it is piggyback on dialectic. Whereas dialectic is the reality of what is going on among the actors on the stage, rhetoric is the commentary on the action and the direct address of the audience. Whereas dialectic lets the audience make up their own minds, rhetoric instructs the audience as to what they're to see and how they're to judge what they're seeing.

Our word "criticism" comes from the Greek root *krisis*, which is the label for the point at which thesis and antithesis join in equal and opposite force. Everything the Greeks did was based on a theory of motion. And so within the dialectic they would say the thesis is an action, an activity, a motion in that direction. Antithesis is motion, equal and opposite, in the other direction. The key question between rhetoric and dialectic is, what do you call this point of clash where the irresistible object meets the immovable force? In dialectic the Greek word is *krisis*. In rhetoric the Greek word is *stasis*.

We must think about *krisis* or crisis the same way we do when we're in a hospital and calling a patient "critically ill." The patient is at the moment of being suspended between life and death. What we do or don't do will conceivably cause the life or death of the patient. It's *krisis*; it's critical. We must make a choice, come to a conclusion. And what we come to is either right or wrong—there are no choices. When we perceive a *krisis*, we have a contradiction. All criticism searches for is contradictions.

If we see a *stasis*, there's no *krisis*; there's a *stasis*, a standing still. When the irresistible force meets the immovable object, they both just simply stop. They can't go any more. We can't move the immovable, and we can't resist the irresistible, so they just simply clash and stop. At that moment we don't have a *krisis;* we have a cessation of motion. And that cessation of motion can only be resolved by judgment. We must make a wise judgment. Now the Greeks have different words for knowledge. If we perceive this as a *krisis,* then the kind of knowledge we're looking for is *episteme,* but if we perceive it as a *stasis* and we're looking for judgment, then the kind of knowledge that we're looking for is *phronesis. Episteme* is translated as "truth" in the scientific sense, demonstrable truth. This becomes wisdom. Provided knowledge that is necessary for good judgment is wisdom. The kind of knowledge that is necessary to elimination is science.

Any theory that advertises itself as critical theory is fundamentally in the debunking business. It is seeking out the clay feet of all heroes, the seams of the apparently seamless, the silences of the apparently democratic. It is looking for hypocrisy, for contradiction, for things that are not what they appear to be. All criticism does that. Hermeneutics is more appreciative, appropriative. It's not seeking the clay feet, but the noble brow of the hero. It's trying to find out what should be imitated, represented, replicated; what constitutes the tradition; what should keep living.

What fascinates me about these two ways of thinking is that it is more like judging whether a glass of water is half-full or half-empty. Both are true. It is like deciding whether this act of power is empowering or dominating. The same judgment is being made in both cases. How do you look at the world? To me, a critic is a pessimist who sees a half-empty glass, and an interpreter is an optimist who sees a half-full glass. They're both studying the same thing, and they're likely going to come to very similar conclusions. As a matter of fact, they're both going to call their way of proceeding "dialectical." But criticism and hermeneutics are quite different animals.

The rhetorician has a stake in this, because the rhetorician operates at the level of praxis. Suppose I'm a practicing president or lawyer of some sort, and I'm schooled in rhetoric, and

I really want to do it right. I can predicate my practice on dialectics, or I can predicate it on hermeneutics, either one. But if I
predicate my praxis on dialectic, I'm going to take actions and
conduct myself in dark ways. The image in my mind is the difference between the Irish and the Black Irish. It's the maudlin, sad,
melancholic kind of rhetoric. Jack Kennedy was an excellent example of this, the Camelot syndrome. He said that we live in a
"long twilight struggle." He had a very fatalistic vision of himself
as a tragic hero. He was a politician who operated on the basis
of dialectic, and you see that in his *Profiles in Courage,* in which
he talked about people who were caught in contradictions, and
they marked their courage by the way they resolveed their contradictions and moved on toward truth. You find other political
leaders who operate on what I would call more of an interpretive stand. And they tend to be, not "happy talk," but more positive. Reagan seems to me to have been that sort.

An entire culture and political system for the last 400–500
years has been based on these oppositions between forces. Nowadays we have feminists and patriarchs. Or we can divide it between labor and management. All of the various political interests
of the social and cultural formations that make up any advanced
industrial state can be characterized as oppositions. It's easy to
become a passionate participant — what Eric Hoffer called a "true
believer." A true believer is someone who can put on a spotted-
owl suit and not understand that you still have to put milk on
the table for the lumberjack's kids. They just don't understand
it. They are so one-sided, they are so partisan, that they are operating as critics. They see *krisis* — a contradiction — between the interests of the lumber company and the interests of the
environmentalists. And when there is a contradiction, the contradiction has to be resolved.

An interpreter and a rhetorician should think differently
about that opposition. They should accept opposition as ordinary, as a matter of course, in the same way that a defense attorney has a community of collegiality with the prosecutor. They
argue against each other, sure, but they have a drink afterward,
and they negotiate before, and they are able to interact with one

another and to live together. It's not a contradiction; it's a *stasis*. And it doesn't exist to be removed or eliminated, it exists to be managed. It must be managed properly.

This principle applies to virtually all political clashes. Too frequently we are encouraged to think about political relationships Platonically, as a sort of dualistic clash between forces, one of which is going to lose and go away. And it doesn't work that way. Losers don't go away. They always come back.

I've said for fifteen years that rhetoric is, and always has been, feminist. If you read rhetoric as being about *stasis* and not about *krisis*, then you are reading the negotiated version as opposed to the win–lose version. The win–lose version is clearly patriarchal, clearly masculine, in its construction in our society. This negotiated version depicts rhetoric as always having been feminine. And it only makes sense because in politics we're trying to construct win–win situations whenever we can. There's a lot of discursive evidence to suggest that politics has been a win–lose game simply in the way we describe elections with metaphors of horse races and sports, and how we feel about our sports teams when they lose. But we shouldn't think of it that way. Everybody wins when there's a game played. We just simply need to construct a world in that way. And we need to construct politics in the same way too, but there's a lot of evidence that we don't. Underneath that verbal evidence, there's still less than a nickel's worth of difference between the two teams or the two political parties. The American political structure is so narrow that it's virtually impossible for us not to have a win–win situation in any kind of an out-and-out political party conflict.

Where we get in trouble in our society is when we do have legitimate clashes, such as the one between right-to-life and freedom-of-choice people. This, to my mind, is a more real political division than any of the political parties. In this dispute, the spectrum is wider than our ability to let it come out win–win. People on the freedom-of-choice side do not want a resolution that will allow right-to-lifers to save face. They simply don't. And the other way around too. I think both the right-to-life folks and the pro-choice folks are operating on a *krisis* model. Judgment is involved, but the issue is whether the state should judge or the individual should judge about when to have an abortion. That's the real issue from an interpretive rhetorical viewpoint. But it's being portrayed in the rhetoric as a situation where there is no judgment—where the right to choose is absolute. Pro-choice folks suggest that it doesn't represent judgment; it represents a human freedom, one of the basic human rights. And, simultaneously, the right-to-life folks represent their position as the most basic human right. What people forget is that the object of every one of these genuine political contradictions is to come up with an interpretation of history, of liberalism, of our culture, and of our community that makes the conflict seem silly. It needs to make settling the conflict so obvious that it seems silly to have engaged in it in the first place. But we're not thinking along those lines. We have to construct things so that the right to this judgment—and the locus of the judgment—the texture and character of this judgment—are obvious, and anyone who couldn't see it beforehand was just ignorant. They just hadn't thought about it enough.

Rhetoric does not assume war. It assumes that conflicts can be resolved. I've studied wars all the way from military tactics on the battlefield to what was said at home on both sides. God is always on both sides in every war. In a war we characterize our enemy as being inhuman—not "us." We create a language about "them," a derogatory language, in order to dehumanize them, to make killing them no more significant than squashing a cockroach. Words like "slope," "gook," and "jerry" construct a fundamental "otherness." When we are at war, it is in effect cutting off a part of our society. It is saying they don't belong. It is saying that they are insignificant, that they are like cockroaches, and we would actually consider killing them. To say that one social formation inside a state is at war with another is to say that the existence of the state itself is threatened.

Because of the destructive potential of technology that virtually all of us have access to, when one social formation is at war with another social formation, we are saying that the life of the world is threatened. I could build an atomic bomb. I really could. I do not have a scientific background, but the material is in our library. It is simply a recipe. I could just cook up an atomic bomb, if I could find the plutonium. But most conflict is not of the war-like variety. And rhetoric assumes that all conflict, even conflict of a war-like variety, can be translated somehow into a rhetorical situation where the conflict can be managed rather than yielded to. Communication understands that there are no differences among people that cannot be bridged. Let's say I go into court and have an incredibly heated conflict over the distribution of property in a divorce. The judge makes a decision. Now I don't walk out and shoot my ex-spouse. The judge made the decision. I live with it.

However, rhetoric is not pacifist in the sense that it is hostile to the use of force. Rhetoric, in a very real sense, is parasitic upon force. It requires the threat of police action, the threat of war, the point of the bayonet, as a way to work its persuasions and to motivate people to come together. It's not pacifistic in that sense. But it is pacifistic in the sense that it always tries to sublimate coercion and to sublimate physical violence whenever possible—to emphasize that after it's all over, we have to live together. We come to the middle.

WISDOM

Unlike philosophers and scientists, rhetoricians have to adapt to the audience. We have to control ourselves, and we have to be right. We do that by doing something that Americans particularly seem to have lost any respect for. It has nothing to do with methods; it goes by an old-fashioned, very respectable word: "judgment." Judgment, not expertise. And we do it by developing the human character, the human quality, that underlies judgment: "wisdom."

What authorizes any criticism is the wisdom of the fragments of the pieces that we put together—what we choose to put together, and whether or not it makes sense. Whether or not people can recognize it as something that for the moment for them is going to pass for the truth.

I need the help of Greek terms when I start thinking of wisdom. The two that I really need are *phronesis* and *deinesis*. The Greeks had quite a reputation among the other people of the Mediterranean, because they were such verbal and philosophically logical people. And they had a reputation for being extremely clever. People might have said, "if you're going to buy a used chariot, go buy a used chariot from a Phoenician or an Egyptian. Don't ever deal with a Greek, because you're going to be taken to the cleaners." And the basis for this was the Greek's mastery of the arts of persuasion, of rhetoric. These arts could be practiced in a purely technical way in order to manipulate, to dominate, and to maneuver in society. The person with this ability would be called a *deinos*. It is Callicles in the exchange in the *Gorgias*. It is the person who has very little moral understanding of his or her life, the culture, or the history, but understands the machinery, the procedures of persuading someone. Contrary to this would be someone who has thought carefully about all of the options that are available and agrees to persuade only when persuaded himself or herself and only in that direction. Here you try to achieve a kind of practical wisdom, or *phronesis*.

For me, *phronesis* is understood in opposition to *deinesis*. What we're after is not the *deinos* but the *phronimos,* the person who is embodied with practical wisdom. Isocrates believed that being a *phronimos* could be taught. It was not a matter of being born to it. The secret was to study the history of one's people. The first step is to understand that there's a connection between who a people were, who they are now, and who they may become. If we've noticed the fact of change in the past, then what has happened can happen. Change can occur in the future. We can envision those evolutions and those changes, and lead our people in that direction. It is the social surgery that Isocrates envisioned in the *Panagyricus,* the *Panatheniecus,* and some of his other treatises.

The learning of wisdom is comparing leaders of today and decisions of today over and against leaders from other countries, and leaders and judgments and decisions from earlier times, so that we understand the history of our people as if it were one gigantic single speech with multiple voices contributing to it through time. And a person's voice contributing to it today could be shrill, or it could be harmonious. It could be in keeping, in patter, in rhythm, as it were—with what has gone before, or it could be against the rhythm, atonal, discontenting in some way. The *phronimos* seeks the rhythm, seeks the continuity. A lot of people interpret that as meaning that a *phronimos* can't be a revolutionary. Habermas has said that Gadamer's thinking, the thinking of a *phronimos,* had in the past led to a kind of fascism with Hitler. But it is kind of silly and stupid to think that revolutions can only proceed from ruptures. Gadamer's point, I think, is more ethical than that. He's not against revolution. He's talking about the kind of revolution that makes sense, that is moral. He wants a revolution that will last and not require moments of domination in order for it to succeed and continue to succeed. What he's suggesting is that dramatic changes can take place.

Isocrates again is an example of a *phronimos.* I can think of no more dramatic change among the Greek city-states than for them to start thinking of themselves as Greek and to stop thinking of themselves as Athenian or Spartan or Theban. Isocrates set this as a persuasive goal for himself: "Reidentify yourself, redefine yourself." And he interpreted history, the leaders, and the decisions of the past to show how it was among the Achaians. There had been in the past impulses to come together, to act as one, to be one people against the Persian threat in the time of the Trojan War, or in any kind of adversity. He showed how developing a national consciousness as Greeks was a very natural next step for the evolution of society.

Now notice, this is making revolution into an evolution. If figured boldly, in terms of a Stalinesque five-year plan, it could be truly rupturous, but the rhetorician doesn't let it stay truly rupturous. A rhetorician is at pains to show how the recommended changes flow from the past. That is, they're a part of an interpretation of what the culture is, and of who the people are, that is consistent—that lets us stay as one people.

I like to look to history for proofs of some of these theories when I can. There have been very few successful revolutions in the world. We've gotten to the point today, I guess, where we call every *coup d'état* a revolution. The French revolution was a bad revolution in rhetorical or Isocratean terms. It gloried in its newness. It rubbed the new in the face of the old. It discredited everything that was past. It didn't flow from anything. The Russian revolution was a bad revolution for the same reason. Both of those revolutions were fundamental failures because of an inability of the new to develop its own sense of tradition, its own sense of roots, its own sense of having come from somewhere and thence going somewhere. The successful revolution in world history has been the English or American revolution.

Of course many revolutionary thinkers, particularly today, don't even like to use the word "revolution" with regard to the American experience; the revolution was too conservative for them. At every stage—from the time of Elizabeth I through the passage of the last British reform bill in 1911, including the American experience with the Revolutionary War and the Civil War—the politicians and intellectuals of the period took a great deal of trouble to explain how the next increment in the emergence of liberalism flowed from and was dependent upon what had come before. In the end, we have a political system that can never be justified by formula, but only by narrative.

Fascism and communism are political systems that we can formalize. They become formulas. We do this because of this rational set of inferences. We organize it this way because of these arguments. We can't *argue* liberalism into existence. We can only *story* liberalism into existence. We have to tell its story from then until now; otherwise, none of the parts fit together. Legal discourse sounds and looks and is totally different from Congressional discourse, which is totally different from what goes on in the churches, and, God knows, how could we have these giant breaches existing in a liberal state? It is just too contradictory. We have to story it in order to get all those contradictions to work together.

Now what does all this have to do with wisdom? The Isocratean claim is that the capacity to ground change in tradition gives people a sense of life greater and longer than themselves, and forces upon them a responsibility to themselves, to the past and to the future, which makes them circumspect in everything that they do. It makes them cautious. It's not an oxymoron to say "cautious revolutionary." It has been made to seem an oxymoron because of the behavior of the French and the Russians in the past couple of hundred years. But revolutions can be worked that are quiet, silent, bloodless, and—to use the English word—"glorious." Even when we have an extremely bloody moment in such a revolution, like the American Civil War, the blood is less important—the dramatic rupture is less important than the continuity. Those who won the Civil War pointed out how their way of thinking of the world was more consistent with the regional ideals of the republic than the way of thinking of those who had lost.

Thematizing and narrativizing give us the big picture. The essence of wisdom is being able to story or to pattern not just the particular issue that's bothering us at the moment, but the history, the coming to be, of the particular problem that is bothering us, and the contextualization of that particular problem with problems that bother other people. Where is wisdom called for? Wisdom is called for when Solomon has two mothers claiming the same baby and has to find out which woman is willing to give up the baby rather than forfeit its life. It is called for where interests clash. It is the ability to see our way through a clash of interests—to make sure that what we do not choose gets its day in the court of our mind.

The *phronimos* is schooled in this because the *phronimos* is first of all a historian, a historical storyteller, someone who is aware of the tradition. Not "Monkey see, monkey do," "Give me that old-time religion," "If it was good enough for grandpa, it's good enough for me." Not that way. But in a way that always tries to ask what the past has to do with the present, and what the past and present together have to do with the future.

Rhetoric is the bridge between ethics and politics. Hermeneutics, or the art of interpretation, is what the rhetorician must know in order to get across the ethics part of the bridge. What we now call "communication" is the politics part of that bridge. The communication side asks how we get the message across. What image should be projected? Which network should we buy air time on? What should be our issues in this campaign? And so forth. Communication today is focused on very practical questions, typically of the hired-gun variety that a communication expert who is practicing politics or involved in Madison Avenue ad campaigns would ask.

The politician must be a *phronimos*. A *phronimos* must be imbued with practical wisdom, must be able to put into practice what he or she thinks is right, and must be able to arrive at what is right with an eye toward putting it into practice. A *phronimos* has to have the attitude that nothing *is; it does*. Such a person has to be interested in consequences, in what happens next. And he or she has to be interested in meanings and understandings.

However, politics is usually frozen in the Cartesian moment. It's *realpolitik*, practical politics, what works. We study the voting patterns, consult the opinion leaders, and all that sort of stuff. It is like Cartesian thinking—the separation of fact and value. Politics simply isn't informed by ethics any longer. Those politicians who are informed by ethics haven't used rhetoric as the bridge, because their ethics are grounded in vital impulses. Most of the environmental movement is this way. The environmental movement is very poorly storied. It's composed of a number of people who have made some vital judgments about their own life and how they live, without understanding how environmental positions and questions and issues are textualized from then until now, and where it might all go.

In Greek, *phronimos* is literally "man," but it means a person who possesses or is imbued with practical wisdom. And this practical wisdom can be taught by giving people a proclivity for thinking in terms of the big picture—for trying to think of intellectual history as something we can actually talk about in conversation. It's something we can do. It's quite different from what it was when I was a kid in graduate school. The history of ideas was bound up in this Johns Hopkins Great Chain of Being notion, and it was intimidating. The idea that a graduate student or a professor could sit down at a table and take an idea from the Greeks to the present in thirty minutes would just offend everyone, because that's not the way the history of ideas worked. But if we're going to have people who are imbued with practical wisdom, we have to be able to do that. We have to be able to give thirty-minute lectures, or sixty-minute lectures, that show how whatever it is we're discussing is connected to intellectual history—where it was, where it is, and where it's going. We've got to story it.

The real problem with practical wisdom is not in teaching it. Teaching it is relatively easy. The difficult part is determining when we've got the genuine article or just something that looks very much like it. In other words, the Callicles or the *deinos* will say something that sounds as if it were an informed practical judgment, when in fact it is a power manipulation. What a person with *deinesis* would say would sound like what a person who is striving for *phronesis* would say. And it also sounds like what a really good used-car salesperson would sound like. We can only test this person if we apply the same standard we would to any witness in a prosecution. Is this person sincere? Does he or she appear to be knowledgeable? Certainly all of these things can be faked. And the *deinos* fakes them. But the claim of the *phronimos* is really to *do* what other people try to put on the *image* of having done

Everyone tries to appear to be a *phronimos*. No parent has ever approached a child having an adolescent problem or having some childhood problem without trying to appear to be wise. (I guess there may be some people who just fly off the handle, but they'll regret it later.) We'll probably wind up telling the kid what we were told. There's no unique advice; we just pass it on. That tells us something about *phronesis* too, in the sense that traditions do matter and count, even in revolutionary personalities, if only because we replicate so many of the behaviors. The kid has to make up his or her mind somewhere along the way. And some kids will go away from home and they'll never go back. Other kids will be amazed at how much smarter their fathers or mothers have gotten in the three years between eighteen and twenty-one.

Learning to imitate *phronesis,* learning to mime it, is easy. Living it is a little harder. We have to go against the grain of our own inclinations. Any time we think that something is absolutely right, we have to argue against it right there on the spot. Check it back, check it back, check it back. Our commitments always have to be, in that sense, rationalized commitments. We can't make a recommendation that we can't narrativize, that we can't story. Coming up with a judgment on the question of abortion is really easy. We've got established sides on the political question, and we all know what the issues are between those sides, and we can say, "I'm over on the left," or "I'm over on the right," or "I'm in the middle," and we've got ourselves oriented. But if we have to make a judgment that matters, that's when it gets hard. Most of us who are on the pro-choice side tell everybody that the issue is not whether or not to have an abortion. The issue is who tells us that we have to or cannot have an abortion. But when it gets down to the actual choice, the judgment that has to be made — a friend of ours has to go through this, or we're going through this ourselves — then it's really hard. It's really hard to put our theories into practice.

REPRESENTATIONS

If we realize that what we're studying is rhetorical, we're going to improve what we know — in social science, in criticism, in social theory, in literature. When we're attempting to study the way people behave or act, we're studying representations. What we're studying is rhetoric. That's the important reason for using the word "representation." The reason we are able to make generalizations about these depictions, any kind of generalizations — whether it's a professor making science, or a critic making criticism of a television show — the reasons we are able to make generalizations is because we recognize that the relationships being depicted are the same relationships that constrain, restrict, control, and influence our own behaviors and beliefs. Every depiction of a preferred social relationship is a re-persuasion, an intense persuasion — an "overdetermination," in Althusser's words — of the same constraint that exists in society. It's a Catch-22. It's a vicious circle.

Television shows are realistic because they portray relations as they exist in society. The portrayal as it exists in society encourages and intensifies those kinds of relationships; it makes them even more normative, more constrictive, and more constraining. It is an elaborate system of a perpetual-motion rhetoric—a rhetoric that constantly reinforces itself, makes itself come true.

The scientistic cause-and-effect formula won't work as a way of studying human communication, because there's no beginning and no end. There's no starting point. It's mirror upon mirror, upon mirror. We live our lives in a hall of mirrors. It's a profound thought that one can distort into the poetry of Baudrillard, but that's basically Baudrillard's point when he's talking about simulacra. We live in a hall of mirrors. He throws up his hands and whines about it a lot, and he says, "I've given up on trying to decide what's the image and what's the real." But I don't think we can do that, because society won't throw up its hands. It's going to tell us what's normal. And as long as society will tell us what's normal, we're either going to give up control of our lives to that definition of "normal," or we're going to figure out what's real on our own. We're going to try to figure out who's making the image.

Every word, every sign, is a theory of its particular usage. In semiotics, if we look up a dictionary definition, this constitutes a theory of that word's usage or a theory of that word's history. And the reason it's still theoretical is that the great uninvestigated morass of semiotics is synchrony—how the words are used, what they mean now, what's going on in the file rather than the rank of the history. But no matter what it says in the dictionary, or no matter what a critic says it ought to be, the Constitution of the United States means exactly what nine old men and women in Washington say that it means in practice. In that sense, the words of the Constitution can't be looked up in a dictionary. They can't be looked up in legal precedent. They're up to the vote of those nine people. Every word is a theory of its actual usage. And its actual usage is what counts.

People in semiotics have developed a series of extremely

useful labels for which they have a scientific understanding. This means that they think they are simply naming the properties of signs, rather than actually studying the history and usage of the signs they're naming and letting the names contain them. Take the term "representation," which is extremely important in semiotics. Most of the important meanings of representation do not derive from the linguistic status of the word "representation." They derive from the use of that term in social and political practice. So, for instance, whenever we talk about representation, the question is never of truth; it's always of authenticity and legitimacy.

Why? Not because of the history of the term, but because of the usage of the term in the context of diplomatic and legal communication. When an ambassador speaks to the President of the United States, or when a lawyer speaks to a court, the court and the President refer to what is said as a representation. They're not concerned with whether it's the truth or not. They expect it to be distorted; it is persuasive discourse, seduction in the direction of the interest of the country or the client represented. But they do expect it to be legitimate and authorized. If it turns out that the country the ambassador represents cannot be held responsible for what the ambassador says, the President is going to be pissed. If it turns out that the client cannot be held responsible for what an attorney represents, the attorney is going to jail for contempt of court. What is missed in semiotics is the question of legitimacy and authenticity—the meaning of the word "representation." Even one of my heroes, the great guru Roland Barthes, misses this dimension of representation. A semiotician would look at the word "representation" more aesthetically. The difference is between a camera photograph and, say, an impressionist painting, or pointillist, or dadaist, or some other kind or style of painting that is not camera, not representation. A representation is different from a sign because a sign is not necessarily representational. A sign consists of a signifier plus a signified. The signifier is like a word or gesture or some other sign, some symbol. And the signified is our idea of what's out there. It's not what's out there.

Basically, semiotics is a radical empiricism. It's the critique

of ordinary scientific empiricism and suggests that a scientist is
never empirical enough. Why? Because we have to talk about the
literal truth of how we observe things. And it is literally true that
in our three-dimensional world we cannot observe all of a thing,
all at once. We have to take a mental photograph of this side,
then that side, then the top, then the bottom. We weigh it. We
do all of the other things we want to do with this object. Then
we put a mental picture together of the dark side of the moon,
the bottom side of the Empire State Building, or whatever it is.
We put the mental picture together so that when we say "Empire
State Building," or "The moon is a sphere," the signified is in our
heads; it's not out there.

Semioticians are the ones who remind us of this fundamental truth. One of the reasons why Saussure and the semioticians
have been so influential in this century is that in the 1950s and
the 1960s it was terribly important to find some kind of a refuta-
tion of scientism, particularly the positivist branch of it, and this
Saussurian linguistics represented a positive, stunning, and telling critique of science. It's a critique from the inside. It's not "I've
got tradition on my side," or "God's on my side," or that kind of
thing. It's not the scientists fighting religious mysticism. It is,
rather, "You guys want to be empiricists? Fine, let's be empiricists. You're not empirical enough. Your observations aren't observations at all. They're always already theorized. They're always
already mental constructions."

In the relationship among sign, signifier, and signified, not
every sign is a representation, because the signified and the sign
are in our heads. When we want to say that the signified should
be "out there," when it's really necessary for us to get a rocket
to Jupiter or talk about real trees, we cannot do that ourselves
except in conversation with ourselves. We do it in *ensimismamiento* — in and beside ourselves. We do it in groups. It takes more
than one people. We sort of "share our signifieds," and we transform what is a signified for any one of us into what is a representation for the group.

A representation is a group meaning. That's why it's very important in the study of culture, and it becomes, in Jameson's

words, a prison house. What we are concerned with, then, are not signs or signifieds but representations. We are concerned with community designation or association of certain meanings with "out-there-ness," and this becomes a representation, a camera photograph. Of course, if we have a camera photograph of something, then we're not authorized to paint the woman blue. We can't do that because it looks like a kid's finger painting, and it's not realistic. And that becomes political pressure on us, which is why the Marxists and the culture critics are so involved in theories of representation.

One of the things that attracts me so much to the ecology movement is that frequently our representations of the earth, even in the sciences, are more about ourselves than about the earth. We're not satisfied with the earth as we find it, or with life as we find it. We insist that it has to be perfect. And it is not perfect until we have perfectly represented it. We invent units of measure — acres, for example — and then we will perceive expanses of land as a quantity of acres and assume that when we're talking about these acres, we're talking about a natural resource. Well, there's nothing natural at all about dividing the earth up into acres. This is a strictly representational phenomenon. It's our rottenness with perfection. We can't just simply say that there's a "whole lot" of land out there. We've got to put a number on it. And we've got to be precise about putting our number on it, and we've got to have a surveyor go out and mark the lines off to the nth degree.

We live in different levels of experience. This is the same thing Foucault is discussing in *Discipline and Punish*. The society does define what realities a normal person will perceive as real. And we are willing, in extreme cases of eccentric perception, to lock someone up in a rubber room and call that person "mentally ill." Most of our judgments in this matter are purely rhetorical, I'm convinced, having read the renegade author Thomas Szasz's delightful book on the myth of mental illness, called *Ideology as Insanity*. He points out that virtually every category of mental illness in the medical profession represents a societal or cultural norm being enforced on deviant people. That's fundamentally Foucault's point when he talks about the madhouses in Europe.

Although there are levels of reality, ultimately there is going to be social or cultural pressure to designate one of them as the privileged or the preferred. We might not like the fact that our perceptions and activities are measured against this cultural, social insistence, but they will be, whether we like it or not.

An example of these levels of experience is television. Here the problem is not with our technical terms or even ordinary language. The problem is with shortcuts that we take in employing those vocabularies. We do experience television. But what it is that we experience is not an *experience*. The television show itself is not experience, but a representation of experience. What we are experiencing with television is not life, but a representation of other experiences. People get confused about this all the time. It's one of the fundamental points of any kind of social critique.

Everyone thinks they know all about hookers from having seen so many cop shows featuring pimps and hookers—so much so that there was an example of this in Los Angeles. A woman successfully defended herself against a charge of common prostitution before a jury on the grounds that she didn't look like a prostitute. She didn't wear clothes or behave anything like they did on television. This is one of the examples I use of Baudrillard's "hyperreality." We make reality conform to representations on television.

Representations are constructed, and this is something that escapes the semioticians. If there's a prison house of language, somebody built the damn house, somebody keeps it in repair, somebody keeps it standing. And that's where the sociological constructionists came along. That's where they get their name. Yes, we're dealing with a representation, but we're dealing with a representation that was constructed, and if we want to understand the experience that it contains, we must first deconstruct it. We must never mistake the representation itself for experience.

For example, I open my wallet up to a photograph and say, "There's my daughter. Isn't she pretty?" This is a terrible error. This is not my daughter; this is a photographic representation

of my daughter. When we look at the *Mona Lisa,* that is an aesthetic experience. We are not seeing the *Mona Lisa.* We are seeing a painting named for the woman who was Mona Lisa, the
woman represented. Through history, there have been men who
get so absolutely fascinated with this woman's face that they fall
in love with her. They are confusing the representation and the
experience. There is a distance between the television character
and a person we would run up against in the mall. If we care
more that the television character was the victim of some injustice
than that a real person we know has been a victim of injustice,
then our values at the very least are screwed up. There are people who live their lives in television. And it is at least obsessive
when this occurs.

Nevertheless, one can have an authentic aesthetic experience
of popular cultural phenomena as easily as one can of high cultural phenomena. Developing personal relationships with people on television is a mark of high-quality television. If we are
aware of parasocial relationships, and if we do inject ourselves
into those sorts of situations, then we become analysts of social
situations on television, and those, although representations, are
more real and authentic than anything else being represented
on television. They have to be, because it is serial television. It
has to be authenticated as realistic by millions of people who
watch it. If our attention is riveted upon relationships among
people and the values that they instantiate, then we're studying
something that's probably the most real thing on television—
more real than the daily news. Every experience of a representation is an authentic experience. There's no question about that.
But if we believe that by virtue of having experienced a representation, we know something about the human beings depicted in
that representation, from a materialist's perspective we're making an error.

Television has a technological capacity that writing and
speaking don't have, and that is the live broadcast. People say
live television is dead, but live television isn't dead; it is confined
mainly to sporting events. Although everyone is accustomed to
the fact that television is capable of live broadcast, it wasn't until

very recent years, with the threat of laws forcing them to do so, that television news organizations put a little print in the corner of the screen that tells you whether it's live or recorded. There's a tremendous possibility for confusion there. It is possible for us actually to be there in live television, and for that experience to be more authentic, more immediate, than to see a newsreel of it at the movie theater or to read about it in the newspaper, or to hear a story about it from someone who was there. However, the vantage point of the camera is never the vantage point of a person, so we have to maintain our distance between witnessing a live event on television and being a spectator at that event in person.

We are privileged in terms of our vantage point if we're watching through a television lens. Furthermore, the television lens is a better technology than the human eye is. I can't zoom, despite what they say in Tom and Jerry cartoons, but a camera can. And even if we're studying a live event, we have to compensate for the advantages that televisual presentations give us. Of course, we aren't getting the smells and the sensual things present when we are actually in a stadium. Everything is reduced to a visual metaphor.

If we're studying formal situations, television is probably the best place in the world to do that because of the commercial nature of the medium. Television does not sell its programs. Television, as Dallas Smythe says, attracts audiences with its programs and sells them to advertisers. In one sense they're in the slave business, and they're out of business if they don't attract audiences. What do audiences demand? Audiences demand drama and laughs from situations that are culturally real for them. By that I don't mean *really* realistic. We've only had two or three working-class representations, actual representations. America's cultural reality is suburban, middle-class. But given that fact, people insist that the relationships they see be realistic. If a love story is being portrayed, they need to be able to project themselves into that situation and say, "Yeah, I could fall for that guy too." If they can't, they won't buy the show.

What we're seeing with the Roseanne Barr phenomenon on

television is a clear example of working-class representation. Roseanne did everything that she could over the past few years to insult and alienate the American people. She grabbed her crotch in public; she sang the national anthem off key; she got the President of the United States to say that he doesn't like the way she sings. This is a woman who has really gone out of her way to rub people the wrong way. And there was some real fear that the ratings for her show would go down. In fact, the ratings for her show skyrocketed. They're even higher now [1991] than they were last year, and she was a star last year. So what's going on? Roseanne is presenting probably the only authentic American family on television.

Her show fills a silence. It has filled a structured absence. Once we leave them out, once we silence them so much that it becomes obvious and evident that we're leaving them out, then what we're not saying speaks more eloquently than what we are saying. When Roseanne Barr gives voice to this silence in her own show, it's immediately recognized as authentic experience by the vast majority of the people who watch television.

Another great example of this was Archie Bunker in the early '70s. America was full of bigots, but we never saw a bigot on television or in film. Even bad guys were bad not because they were bigots, but for other reasons. So we had a whole American society that was convinced that we needed to get rid of racism and bigotry, but everybody was asking themselves the same question and nobody was saying in public, "What are we going to do with the bigots in my family? What am I going to do with Uncle Joe? What am I going to do with my dad?" And Archie Bunker gave us a way to deal with that. Archie Bunker gave us a buffoon in a sense, and we could now place Dad. Now at the supper table we could be honest. We could say, "Oh, damn, Dad, you sound just like Archie Bunker. Shut up and eat your supper."

No matter how complex our communication technologies and industries become, it is literally impossible for them to represent all of America, even if all of us get our own shows. There are margins forever. It is a matter of size. It's inherent in the whole notion of representation. The French have been harping on the notion of presence and fullness for twenty years. The fact that you are representing something silences something else. Our communication research people tell us that there are two and a half kids in the American family. I've never seen a half kid. And just because a lake averages six inches in depth doesn't mean you can't drown in the middle. Every generalization silences the particular.

Because television is a commercial enterprise, the formal situational representations in television are a good thing to study — not because they are the experiences themselves, but because they are an interesting example of the form of that relationship in reality. Television gives us accurate representations. It is art capturing the truth of the matter. The error is really one that Baudrillard points out, and that's the error of hyperreality. The error is when we dismiss things that we are immediately and personally experiencing on the grounds that what we are immediately or personally experiencing does not conform to what we know from our televisual experience.

One of the earliest and most interesting experiments along this line was done by Allen Funt in the context of an old popular television show, *Candid Camera*. He also had some theatrical releases, which allowed him to be a bit more risqué in his films than he could be in his television show. The first film that he made on the basis of *Candid Camera* was *What Do You Say to a Naked Lady?* He was testing violation of pattern of expectations with regard to psychological perceptions. He rigged up an office building in Detroit so that one elevator in a bank of elevators opened up to a beautifully proportioned blonde in a very skimpy bikini, with fake theater smoke made from dry ice coming up from the bottom of the thing. A shower head had been implanted, and what one saw was a naked lady taking a shower.

Now four things happened. A few people said, "What? Am I on *Candid Camera?*" We would say these people had their heads screwed on straight. We would say they were very smart, very perceptive. People in Illinois would say they were cognitively complex. They were special in some way. They were not going to be fooled by hyperreality. Another group of people weren't going to be fooled by the naked lady either. They didn't know they were on *Candid Camera,* but they had an accurate perception of what they saw. They thought, "I saw a woman in a bikini, and there was some smoke from dry ice coming out, looked like steam of some sort. Somebody really screwed around with that elevator." A third group immediately removed her bikini and thought she was naked. These people redefined what they saw to fit the world of possibilities. They saw a naked lady taking a shower. A fourth group said, "It didn't happen. I didn't see anything. Did you see something? I didn't see anything." They discounted what they saw. They may have truly convinced themselves that they didn't see anything.

Everyone has an understanding that he or she can be fooled, deceived; that he or she can go crazy; that aberrant behavior, aberrant perceptions are possible. We all know that. And one of our reactions, whenever we know that we are in this kind of situation, is to pretend that it didn't happen. Pretend that we didn't see it. We think we see a ghost, and the last thing we ever say is "I think I saw a ghost." We just stay away from there for a while and keep it to ourselves. "I didn't see a flying saucer. I was coming home last night at 9:00 P.M. and I didn't see a flying saucer."

We all make judgments on the basis of patterns of expectations that we develop through our personal life experience. If we start making those sorts of judgments on the basis of televisual experience, we are in the world of hyperreality, and we have a problem. And Baudrillard is absolutely right about that. In other words, if we let television and not our lives in everyday praxis establish our patterns of expectations about what the truth is—so that we are willing to ignore the reality of homeless people, the reality of prostitution, or whatever else we're talking about, in favor of our understanding of televisual representations of it—we are in the world of hyperreality, and we have a real problem.

When Baudrillard talks about the postmodern condition and the emergence of hyperreality, he's not talking about a universal human response to new technology. Hyperreality is a major social problem only for the third and the fourth categories of people I was talking about earlier—for the people who pretend that there is nothing there, and for the people who remove the bikini. If I can distort reality, if I can make the woman naked, then hyperreality is a problem. And if I ignore something in reality, it's a problem. But if I say, "Am I on *Candid Camera?*" or give an accurate description of what I've seen, there's no problem.

Chapter Three

The Postmodern Condition

Every generation of graduate students has its own Derrida, its own outrageous thinker, and in the 1960s the outrageous thinker was Marshall McLuhan. I was always fascinated by Marshall McLuhan, and I read everything that he wrote. And for the most part, I did not approve of it. But there are two things that I learned from McLuhan that I do approve of. One is the necessity to take a broad historical view of the development of cultures. We frequently don't do this because we have been educated into a sort of pseudoscientific mentality—to approach the history of ideas very methodically, as a matter of influence, one linked to the next link in the Great Chain of Being, as A. L. Lovejoy would have it. We frequently get bogged down in the history of ideas to the point where we can't see the forest for the trees.

For instance, we had in rhetorical studies in the 1960s historians of rhetorical theory writing essays on the influence of some minor rhetorician you'd never heard of on another minor philosopher you'd never heard of, whose work Joshua Reynolds read that influenced the way he painted pictures. This sort of work was fascinating from a detective story viewpoint, but if I want a mystery story I'll read Agatha Christie. McLuhan is a good corrective for this, in that he doesn't want to supplant or replace the "history of ideas" notion or any sort of detailed cultural literacy about the history of ideas. But he wants us to take a broad view of the history of ideas, so that we are thinking about how epochs and time spans measured in millennia, rather than in months, weeks, or years, fit together.

The second lesson that I learned from him that I think is very important, and really is underemphasized in Kenneth Burke, is the whole question of technology. Burke claims to have written more about technology than I think he actually did. McLuhan wants us to look at the interactions between ideas and technology, and how some ideas are virtually identical with the technology that makes them possible, in the sense that the medium is the message. Burke wants us to believe that scientific technologies are the big problems of this century, and that they make most of the political ideologies unacceptable accountings of the state of culture in the contemporary world. But he doesn't really get down to the impact of technology on the flow of history, or the role technology has to play in our deciding what constitutes an epoch, and how one period of time fits with another period of time.

We put those two ideas together with my own specialty, which is the study of communication, and with the now-popular notions about *l'écriture* in French discourse theories and the importance of writing, and I think some really interesting possibilities can occur. I came up with the tale that is a reading of Derrida through the skeptical lenses provided by one who has studied McLuhan and Burke—their agreements and disagreements—with some care. When you think about that, then, you understand that McLuhan is right: that we can characterize the ages of humanity as, if not determined by, then at least reflective of, prevailing communicative technologies.

ORALITY

One of the things that set the ancient world apart from the Renaissance world was the predominance of oral cultures, where speaking and the things that are possible through speaking were the centers of cultural life. In order to escape the handicaps and problems that we had in speaking, we invented technologies. Speaking goes by in a moment, and until very recent years with video technology and film, there was no way to record speech. So we had to have incredibly acute skills of memory.

As I tell the story, and as I read other people like Walter Ong and Marshall McLuhan telling a similar story, the claim has been thus far that orality is the state of nature for us. It is the beginning point. Although we could talk about orality as a technology, because there was once in dim history a time when we made meaningful grunts and invented language, that's so prehistoric that we really can't consider it. Most writers—McLuhan, Ong, and I included—would take orality as the state of nature, the starting point, the beginning place.

Understanding is more important than truth in an oral culture. It doesn't matter to me whether my audience agrees with what I have to say. I'm very flattered that they'll listen to me. In other words, truth is not a consideration in our conversation, but understanding is a consideration. I will go out of my way in terms of being more elaborate, coming back and finding new examples to make sure that my audience understands. Truth doesn't matter as much in an oral culture because it's not possible. It's hard to say something that's permanent. We aim for a version or a kind of truth that our technologies of recording and remembering are up to. With the equipment we're born with—our tongues and our ears and our inventions of language—the kind of truth that an oral culture is up to is the truth of understanding, *verstehen.* The invention of writing, I believe, can be characterized as a response to the gravest and most glaring weakness of oral communication: its impermanence.

Writing records what is said, but writing is just a technology of recording. When I read the arguments of some of the most brilliant writers of intellectual history, I find it starkly amazing that the inventor of philosophical thinking, Plato, engaged in an unmistakable diatribe against writing in the *Phaedrus.* It was a new technology at the time of Plato. There are rumors that Plato himself could not read or write, that he had slaves who did this for him, and that he composed his dialogues by dictation. To find someone who was such a consummate master of the new technology—I mean, the man was putting dialogue into writing—at the time that he was condemning writing strikes me as a remarkable contradiction.

What he was doing was calling attention to the limitations of the technology in much the same way that I might get up in a classroom today and caution people that a computer program is not intelligence, or caution people that a televisual representation of a social relationship is not a social relationship. He was cautioning people about mistaking or confusing the technology for something that it was not. And he was still afflicted by the old constitution, in a sense, the old way of doing business. His notion of truth, for example, was basically rational, consistent understanding. It was dependent upon dialogue. And the importance of writing was that it could replicate the dialogue.

Replicating and recording the dialogue, technologically, preserved something of the dialogue. But we ought never to confuse the representation of dialogue (i.e., what Plato was writing down in the *Phaedrus*) with the dialogue itself, which is what is being recorded by this technology. So he perfectly well understood the technological nature of writing, and Plato wrote about it and treated it as if it were a technology of writing. He was not up to the new visions of truth that the technology permitted. He was still handicapped by old visions of truth—truth that is really understanding.

Our vision of truth that is something more than what redundant oral communication is capable of is really a product of the next epoch in intellectual history, which is defined by the emergence of the Christian revolution. Early parts of the Torah and the *Enuma Elish,* which is the old Babylonian myth of the creation, were products of an oral culture. They were passed down from generation to generation to generation. But somewhere along the line, priest classes wrote them down, and when they wrote them down they changed the way they talked about them.

Biblical scholars, for example, will look at the books of the Torah and clearly identify different personae or writers, designating those who came from the oral tradition of the religion as "J" writers or "Jahvistic," and those who came from the written-down portion of the religion as "P" for "priestly."

The story of the Garden of Eden is a "J" story from the oral tradition. God is a character who gives voice and has words to say to Adam and Eve in the Garden. The myth of Adam and Eve that Adam understood—in other words, *truth,* with regard to his conduct—was a matter of *understanding*: understanding what God was saying to him in dialogue. That is the same kind of understanding that exists in an oral culture.

The other kinds of truth in the book of Genesis and other parts of the Bible, the "P" versions, are more canonical. They depend upon a social institution that is already there—a church, as it were, or a temple—with assigned job classifications for priests who have a defined relationship to the people that they are priests for and those who are in charge of the government. There is a different accounting of what constitutes truth even in the Hebraic Bible. Here The Word is emphasized. They capitalize "Word." The Word. The writing of The Word in this conception, a "writing" conception, was sufficient to the act of creation itself. This God didn't interact with these people. This God didn't come to the Garden of Eden or anywhere else to talk to humanity. This God appeared, if at all, to selected individuals on the tops of mountains or in the form of a burning bush. And when there was dialogue that was attributed to God, The Word of God, it was not dialogue; it was edict, it was pronouncement. "Thou shalt not," the Ten Commandments say. "Get thee behind me, Satan" is the Christian replaying of the burning bush myth of the old Torah.

There is a pretty clear marker that things were changing with the writing down. The interesting thing is that Christianity as a revision of Middle Eastern religions came at about the same time with regard to the importance of the technology of writing that we were in at the first half of this century—I'd say at about the radio period of writing.

A new nature of truth came about from what I am now call-

ing the age of writing, and it could be called a dialectical circumscription of the truth. In this way, one would argue the same thing
both dialogically (the forms appropriate for understanding) and
according to priestly form (or by edict, or prescription, or dictation—a kind of a written form of logic). And what constitutes
a complete demonstration is a dialectical circumscription of these
two meanings of truth, which would work out to be what the
Greeks called *episteme* (truth as a kind of scientific knowing) and
phronesis, or interpretation, or understanding (which is truth in
a dialogic form).

But we came through the Middle Ages after the Christiani-
zation of Rome, and by the time we got to the Renaissance, it
was virtually impossible to think of anything as truthful that was
not in writing. We developed all sorts of aphorisms and common
places of social and cultural interaction, such as "Get it in writing." Old aphorisms that were associated with orality, like "I have
your word," came into disuse or acquired different meanings.
"Having someone's word" after a certain period of time meant
that you had a written contract. This fetishization of writing, in-
cidentally, continues so much into the twentieth century that we're
getting to the point now where we don't even allow an oral contract in courts of law any more. Requirements of what makes an
oral contract are getting so increasingly strict that such a thing
is virtually impossible to plead by. In this period we came to think
of the written representation of truth as truth.

Notice what a difference this is. Instead of truth lying in the
dialogue, in the agreement among human beings, we locate truth
outside human beings in something that is on the printed page—
something objective, accessible to criticism. This is the move, I
believe, that is more decisive than the quarrel about how many
angels can dance on the head of a pin. This is about signification and nominalism. It is really more important than Cartesian
and Baconian insights about "If you want to know how many teeth
are in a horse's mouth, go count." Those are common sense, and
undoubtedly they were brilliant and important at the time.

What really created objectivity was writing. And writing puts
things "out there," apart from human beings in a material or

pseudomaterial way. If we look at oral treatises, legends, tales that came down in the oral tradition — the *Iliad,* the *Odyssey,* the *Enuma Elish* of the Babylonians, the Torah of the Hebrews, manuscripts that are clearly and undeniably texts from oral traditions — I have never seen a representation of objectivity as a criterion of truth in any of these texts. Truth is instead represented in these oral literatures as a function of someone who has access to special powers. Knowledge is taken from the gods. It is a matter of inspiration. It is divine. It is the spark. It is an implantation of some sort from some divine entity. This divine entity is alleged to be powerful, and the truth of the spark of knowledge depends upon the power of the divinity or the source of the knowledge.

In these old oral texts, knowledge and truth are things of a wholly different order than after the technology of writing is invented. They're dependent upon power; they are instantaneous; they are moments of insight. And I can imagine how this develops. Have you not been in a conversation where you just talk on and on about something that gets you excited, and then all of a sudden a "truth" occurs to somebody? Like the old commercial for Ford, where the light bulb clicks — Ford has "a better idea." That's exactly what it feels like: click, "Oh, yeah, that's it." Well, this is an oral understanding of truth. This sort of thing happens. And in the old myths, that's exactly how they characterize truth and knowledge occurring: "Oh, yeah!" There's nothing methodical about it. There's nothing objective about it. It's rational. It occurs in a rational process, and you can rationalize it. You can explain why it happened and why you believe it once it occurs to you. But that flash of occurrence, that "Oh, yeah!" — *that* was their understanding of truth. How dramatically this changes with the technology of writing.

What's called the Enlightenment is usually considered to be identical with the Age of Reason. What I'm suggesting is that the Age of Reason or the Enlightenment is the heart or the fulcrum of this period where most of the fateful decisions were made. One of them was the "fetishization" of writing, and people came to love and trust their writing and to trust only in writing as they once trusted each other and trusted themselves. All of the characteristics that Barthes and Derrida complain about with regard to writing have emerged at this point. Our truths are already disembodied. It no longer matters that *I* am the one who believes this. It only matters that this is there to be believed. My truths are disenacted. There's a distance between writing and performing, so that I can conceive theory and I can put things into writing that enjoy the important privilege of being mere writing, that aren't put into practice yet. This is what I call the fetishization of writing: when one comes to believe that one lives in writing, that human life and human culture and human states and human ideologies and human values can only be mediated in and as writing.

The great cultural handicap that we have given ourselves is a virtual inability to imagine being human except through mediations. And it starts by the gradual inability to think of ourselves as able to tell the truth or engage in social relationships or entertain ourselves or do art, except where writing or mechanical reproduction is somewhere involved in this process. We haven't escaped that yet.

TECHNOLOGY

Our new technologies allow us the possibility of returning to more oral views of the world. But we're not there yet. Right now, we're transforming all of the prejudices that we once held with regard to writing to other media. We once described the brain in terms of a *tabula rasa* to be written upon. Now we find the same sorts of people making the same sorts of arguments, drawing the comparison between the brain and a computer. The human brain is a computer made of electrical circuits, alpha and beta waves, and it makes binary decisions, "yes" and "no," and comes to conclusions. Then we can make a machine that thinks like the human mind, because we can create electronic circuitry that mimics the electronic circuitry of the brain. This is passing now as good science, just in the same way that we believed that the empirical move was good science — that writing it down made it true. And what we keep forgetting is that it's not the writing down that makes it true. And it's not the ability to make a machine that has electronic circuits that imitate the human brain that makes it true. Truth resides in a fully embodied and enacted human practice. *We* are necessary for our own truths.

In the Age of Writing and the Age of Computers, this is going to be dismissed as sheer subjectivity, sheer relativism, the most abject form of relativism possible. But what we have lost through the fetishization of writing is the notion that people are involved in some way in the truths that they possess. As long as we have descriptions of epistemology or descriptions of culture and human society that are imprisoned in writing, or imprisoned in computer technology, or in televisual circuitry, we are simply replicating old mistakes. This is why I say that we could just reverse the polarity. It was the Age of Reason that called the later stages of the oral culture a Dark Age. And if we value humanity and the human element in truths and beliefs, we could reverse that polarity entirely. We could think of the Age of Reason as one long Dark Age where we forgot how to dialogue and forgot the sense in which our truths are necessarily understandings more than writings.

This conception of disembodied truth is a human invention — a by-product of the technology of writing. Once we gain a new technology, we don't lose old technologies. We can make videotape now, but we still write and put a lot of emphasis on writing. We still talk and put a lot of emphasis on talking. We still make films and put a lot of emphasis on films. Technologies relate to one another in an accretion, not by means of replacement. When writing was invented as a technology, it added to our media capabilities. It added another dimension to orality. But it changed the old mode of communication and some of the ideas associated with orality by making it possible for us to speak about objectivity.

One can use media of communication to accomplish anything, in principle, that all the other media can. Some writers can paint pictures in words that are at least as vivid as pictures that cinematographers show us in films. At least in principle, or by figuration, any medium of communication is up to what any other medium of communication can do, at least to a lesser order or to a lesser degree. But each technology of communication that we have invented carries with it certain cultural, philosophical, and rhetorical baggage that we frequently are not aware of. We invent things other than technologies when we invent technologies.

When we invented the system of numbers to the base ten, we invented zero. We were able to think nothing. We did that in arithmetic discourse in the West. In all of the volumes of the *Bhagavad-Gita,* there are all these huge pages that are devoted to trying to comprehend nothing. It didn't come out of the language of arithmetic. Buddha posed riddles and conundrums and paradoxes like "Imagine the sound of one hand clapping." And in order to get at nothing, one had to enter transcendental meditative states and hum mantras. "Put everything out of your mind. Blank white. The world is white." These are two cultures that were able to conceive of nothing — one very easily and rationally, the other with a great deal of difficulty and mysticism. Now what's the difference? There was a technology in the Western society — the invention of a language of arithmetic, a number system to the base ten — that was absent in the East, where they did not have a number system to the base ten. They were counting things up on abacuses with eighteen rows. Every technology of communication that we develop has certain unintended consequences. Sometimes these consequences are good; sometimes they're bad. Usually they're both good and bad. My claim is that the technology of writing invented objectivity. We invented objectivity at the same time that we invented writing. I can see that this has had good and bad consequences. Without some notion of objectivity, we would not have been able to make other machine technologies to get us to Jupiter or to make war on the Iraqis.

Every new technology is going to be accepted by a portion of society and resisted by a portion of society. There are going to be those who will readily go out and get a smallpox vaccination, because now they can resist smallpox. There will be those who won't because they think vaccination is the work of the devil. There is always a polarity of people who oppose and accept new technologies. There's always going to be an argument about those technologies, about how they fit in human cultural forms and human traditional practices. It's been our history that every new technology has been argued for and ultimately accepted. Those who are arguing for a new technology do what any advocate does: They become one-sided; they become biased. If I'm hired to defend somebody in a court of law, by the time I get before that jury, I really believe my case. And I believe it intensely. I will distort reality. I will distort the evidence, unconsciously, in the intensity of my feeling to get my client off in this matter. Advocates are the same anywhere. So those who are in favor of the technology will make slightly more elaborate claims for it than it really justifies. It will be more momentous, more labor-saving, more world-changing than it would be if they weren't opposed by someone who didn't like the technology. It's in the context of this dialogue about how the technology is to be used, sold, integrated into the economy and in cultural practices that the impulse for fetishization works itself out. Because those who are in favor of a new technology always win. Our image of the new technology is their rhetorical hyperbole of it, not the thing itself. It is always mediated.

The difficulty is not that technology puts a person on the moon. I'm all in favor of that. Rockets to Saturn, *Star Wars,* here we come. There's no problem with technology in terms of its product. The difficulty is that technology and science are used as the model for all human knowledge. We all have been accustomed or conditioned to hold ourselves up to the standards that are used in the natural sciences for what counts as knowledge. The difficulty with science is not what scientists do, but with the fact that humanists gave up on themselves. They began to believe that the scientists were more valuable than they were because scientists could make air conditioners and light bulbs, and all humanists could do was find a new way to read Plato, or maybe write a great American novel, or something unimportant like that. What humanists have done is to redefine what counts as knowledge, and what counts as cutting-edge theory that people should be involved with, according to a scientistic model.

What strikes me about European discourse theorists, almost to the person, is that they talk about oral language in the most glowing terms. Written language is constraining; oral is liberating. Written language is binding; oral language is fleeting, temporal. Written language is impersonal; oral language takes account of the personalities who are using it. Written language is disembodied and disenacted; oral language is fully embodied and fully enacted. Every bad thing they say about writing, they say in contrast to speaking, and imply that speaking is almost a regulative ideal of discourse. They're using the qualities of oral discourse in order to blame written discourse. But the irony is that none of them study oral discourse; they all study writing. Only Appel and Habermas are even investigating the possibility of studying orality and theorizing a communicative praxis.

Paul Ricoeur still says that hermeneutics depends on a written text. And when you apply interpretive principles to speeches or anything else, you're applying interpretive principles to something that's been written down. It's the written-down nature, the diachronics, the *la langue* principle that underwrites all of hermeneutics. One of the most respected hermeneutes, Charles Taylor, the great Canadian philosopher, defines hermeneutics as the analysis of texts or text analogues. And by "texts" he means "written."

But rhetoric is a premodern notion associated more with oral cultures than Enlightenment ones. This whole theory of discourse we continue to study today, called "rhetoric," comes from classical Greece. It comes from an oral culture, before the technology of writing had been invented and before human beings fetishized the technology of writing. We can make the assumption, then, that the so-called postmodern, post-Enlightenment, anti-Enlightenment condition that we are allegedly either in or drifting toward today has more in common with the premodern age before the invention of writing than it does with the modern period, because neither the postmodern nor the premodern age fetishizes writing as a technology. The function of the new technologies and the new thought is to explode the feeling of perm-anence or of guarantee that one gets when one "gets it in writ-ing," and to promote the uncertainties and the feeling of the provisionalness of communication that one gets with oral com-munication in the premodern period or with electronic commun-ication today.

We have what is called in hermeneutics an "anagogy." We have a possibility of a historical comparison of two ages, two epochs, such that what happened in the previous epoch can in-struct us as to what's happening in the following epoch, without our need to argue perfect historical parallels. One has to under-stand that premodern and postmodern conditions are not iden-tical. They are merely anagogical. They are commensurable in the sense that there is a common condition for comparison. Pre-modern understandings of society and culture are not commen-surable with the Enlightenment. And postmodern conceptions of society and culture are not commensurable with Enlighten-ment conceptions. But premodern and postmodern conceptions are commensurable with one another. And it is precisely on this basis that we are rejecting the atomistic or scientistic attitude toward human symbol-using behavior, and we are going back in-stead to grammatical, rhetorical, and mathematical relationships as the fundamental units of meaning.

If that's the case, much of the age of simulacra—the "hyper-reality" that Baudrillard and others talk about—was actually a phenomenon in the ancient world too. But there it went under the name of "myths" and "superstitions," where people were so convinced of the truth and reality of the tales about the gods in Olympus and about the legends of the Trojan War that they were willing to measure life occurrences in their experience against the behavior of heroes and gods in what we know of as purely literary adventures. Hyperreality was as much a part of the an-cient world as it is of the postmodern world.

The idea that enabled people to deal with the hyperreality of the world in ancient Greece was rhetoric. Rhetoric was the discipline or the art that walked the line between the arts on the one side and the sciences on the other—between the stories of the religion and the stories of the practical real world that have to be told as we conduct politics and carry on marketplace activities. A twentieth-century rhetoric must be available as a response to the postmodern condition. A postmodern theorist like Baudrillard, for example, is increasingly drawing himself up tight into a little tower of elitism, where he's suggesting that the world is going to hell in a handbasket and all that's left for us to do is laugh as the devil has his way. There's nothing to do about it. Every effort we make to cope with the postmodern condition is bound to end in failure of some sort. There's no way to recoup the situation.

This feeling of failure and nihilism comes from a contradiction in Baudrillard, and that is Baudrillard's acceptance of the conceptions of what constitute reason and rationality in the Enlightenment period, even as he rejects the truth and validity of the claims that reason made about the world. If we rethink reason and think of reason through a rhetorical version of rationality—that is, in contingent matters, given this situation as we understand it, for the moment, and for now; reasoning that takes place in those situations, as opposed to reasoning that demonstrates the truth now and forever in a sort of rationalistic, Cartesian way—then it is possible for us to face the postmodern condition and to deal with it rationally (i.e., rhetorically). To the extent that rhetoric is rational, we can be rational about the simulacra in our world in the same way that the ancient Greeks were rational about the simulacra in their world. The postmodern condition gives us a chance, an opportunity, to say things differently—to phrase traditional problems in a different way, and in a way that invites a different class or category of conclusions.

One thing that Barthes, Derrida, Ricoeur, and Foucault all have in common is that in order to explain the connection between discourse and society, culture, and politics, they have to show the sense in which discourse is somehow decisive and determinate. And their strategy in showing how discourse is so important has been to emphasize the abidingness and the permanence of the written language. If we have a term, it is defined in a particular way in all of the dictionaries; a record of its usage and a history of its usage are all laid out for us. In writing, we have a constitutive or constitution of the word—what it must mean, what it should mean, what we're not free to do with it.

In speaking, on the other hand, we treat words more cheaply than that. When we start talking about the meaning of a word, we begin with a general definition; then we trade synonyms for a little bit. And once we trade synonyms, we'll trade situations and applications. "You mean it's like . . . ?" "No, it's more like . . . " "Oh, I get it, it's like . . . " "Yeah, you're getting it, but really, a little bit more . . . " And we trade synonyms; then we trade circumstances and applications, so that in the speaking of the word, the word itself is actually cheapened. But as we read it in a sentence, my God, it's engraved in stone. Here is the word that I don't understand in that sentence. This whole idea, this whole page, this whole discourse comes down to the fact that I don't understand this word. But if we're in conversation, the fact that you don't understand the word that I'm using causes me not to use it. I'll express the ideas some other way; I'll use other articles; I'll just slip right on past it. It is eminently expendable. When a word is written, it becomes something of a prison house. It becomes binding in a way that oral words aren't.

In the British House of Commons, for instance, they had political rules that enforced an oral culture on the legislative assembly. Originally, it started that they didn't want to put anything in writing that could be used in a court of law against them if the King wanted to prosecute them for some reason. But they passed this rule that you couldn't take notes in the House of Commons, and this held for a number of years through the eighteenth century. You could be thrown in jail for sitting up in the gallery and writing down what people were saying.

With the development of newspapers in England, this created a real market conflict. People needed to know what was going on in government, and they could sit in the gallery, but they couldn't take notes. So they hired a fellow with an eidetic memory for sound, and his name was John Williams. They called him Memory Williams. He would sit in the House of Commons and come back out and replay word for word what went on. And they could take notes of Williams outside the House of Commons, and then they would print what went on.

In England, it has been a matter of great urgency in their political evolution toward democracy that constitutions and rights not be written down. Every law that is passed in Britain is considered to be a *part* of the constitution—not subordinate to the constitution, not done on its authority, but to be a *part* of the constitution. Every British Parliament that repeals a law or changes a law is changing the constitution. To change the franchise in England—say, they want to let fifteen-year-olds vote— all it takes is a majority in the House of Commons. To decide that you ought to have ten million pounds' worth of property before you can hold public office, all it takes is a majority in Commons to decide to do that too. Commons is a tyrant in a sense, from an American perspective, because Commons has all this power that is rigidly controlled by our Constitution—our written document.

In the United States, a legislature passes a law, and at the time you are getting ready to put pen to paper to write a law, one of the big things that is on your mind—whether it's in the city council, or the state legislature, or the House of Representatives—is, will it be constitutional? In other words, will it really be law once we pass it, or will a court review it and throw it out? In England, then, the constitution is lived in a way that it is not here. Every member of the House of Commons is instructed in the history of England, and the history of England is presented fundamentally as the constitution of England. The constitution means the body politic, the narrative sense that understanding our story as a people would be if we could write it all down, all of a piece. They are set up as constitutional interpreters. Every one of them is trained to make decisions historically. On both sides of the aisle: history—precedent—rules. If you are going to move your party or policy against precedent, you have to have real good reasons, and real good reasons in light of a common group consciousness that what is happening is a change in the constitution. So in a sense, England looks very conservative in many ways—very tyrannical. But look at a lot of the liberal reforms that passed in England thirty years before they emerged and developed in the United States.

I think Fredric Jameson was fundamentally right in *The Prison House of Language*. When you write something down, it does indeed restrict your interpretive parameters. If your job is as an interpreter, and if what you are interpreting is a people's understanding of history, your job is entirely different than if what you are interpreting is a written constitution with a Bill of Rights. There are some interesting differences within Anglo-American liberalism as to where the ideographs reside, based in part on a difference between writing and speaking; based in part on the difference between parliamentary and bicameral operationalizations of the republican principle; and based in part on the presence, in the case of Canada, of a very, very strong and intellectually adept French subculture.

John Dewey said that the reason for the decline and fall of the public was the fragmentation of the culture. This has been a point that has been made through most of this century: that we are becoming fragmented as a culture. That we were once a homogenous culture may be questionable, I grant that. But at one time we *thought* we were a homogenous culture, and one of the characteristics of the twentieth century is that gradually over the course of the century we have come to discover that we are a heterogenous culture, and that's what we believe we are. And that marks a dramatic change.

I can't think of anything that it doesn't affect. In 1900, you couldn't go to school in the United States unless you spoke English. Today you have the federal courts requiring education in Spanish and English. At the turn of the century in Canada, you couldn't go to school unless you spoke English. Now it's an officially bilingual country. French is one of the national languages. Suddenly you are introducing the entire literature of the French language as permissible for quotation and citation in public speeches and in newspapers. A whole pantheon of historical figures that are virtually silenced, because they are French and not English, are suddenly given voice. It changes the flavor of discourse. When you get down to something as rudimentary and as basic as the language that one speaks, how can it be doubted that the culture has fragmented? Once you start from this fundamental truth, you then go to the next step, and you say that texts have fragmented correspondingly.

THE TEXT

Our technologies of communication have created a plethora of texts and text fragments that act in various ways upon us, all of them requiring interpretation and criticism. As a result, the traditional roles of speakers and audiences have virtually shifted. They've virtually reversed themselves. In the past, we've put our emphasis on teaching performance, and it was the speaker or the writer who was involved in constructing a text. That was what he or she was all about. Speakers or writers say their own things. It's a free market of ideas, and we choose what we like, and we reject what we don't.

Of course, we are all both communicators and audience members, and our roles shift back and forth between these two jobs of text interpretation and text production. But in the twentieth century the roles have reversed, so that when we are playing speaker, our primary job is interpretation: interpretation of the environment, interpretation of politics, interpretation of the multiplicity of messages that are being received. Whenever we construct, we're involved in producing a speech. We're really manipulating and maneuvering and matching little fragments of texts from here and there—constructing it in a way that says, "Here, see, I've made sense of the world."

We are making discourse, but the primary engine of that discourse's coming to be has to do with the way we interpret the environment and select the fragments that make up what we say. We no longer have the old series of political speeches on the stump or on the Fourth of July, where we have eight or ten speakers, and they each say their say, and then we have a picnic and go home. That was probably the only sort of discourse other than the penny newspaper that a person consumed during the week in the nineteenth century. The only text everyone had in common that everybody quoted from was the Bible. But today people are just being bombarded with so many messages and so many texts—the free market of ideas is so full, so overflowing, and so inconsistent—that the primary business of an audience member any more is just simply figuring out what's being said, simply *understanding*. We have to construct a text in such a way that it makes sense.

This leads me to ask the question: What is a text? We have treated it so frequently as self-evident. Here's American literature. Or here's British literature. And there's Charles Dickens. And clearly *The Pickwick Papers* is a text, but it doesn't work that way any more. Today more people are "reading" television than reading books. And Horace Newcomb has pointed out for years that there's a real problem in deciding what constitutes a text on television. When we focus on Mary Tyler Moore, we are suggesting that what people in the audience are watching is *The Mary Tyler Moore Show*. Well, that's clearly not true. They're watching a series of commercial texts that are interspersed in this literature. Are they watching a single episode of Mary Tyler Moore, or are they watching it through a whole season? Or through a whole career on television? Or are they seeing Dick Van Dyke's wife evolving into Mary Tyler Moore? Or are they watching—and this was Horace's point—are they watching a strip? If we want to make some inferences about the audience, should we understand the text as consisting of all of the programs and commercials that they watch in a particular sitting on television? At 7:30 I watch ABC, and then I switch to NBC, and then I switch back and forth. The text actually becomes what I watched during a given period, rather than any particular thing that's available to be watched.

What we must look at is a new and different kind of speaker. We are now being spoken by "Discourse," written with a capital "D," rather than being spoken by a rhetor. What this means is that the speaker is hidden as the persona of that multiplicity of fragments of discourses that have the effect of constituting us as a people. In the eighteenth century, we could point rather simplistically to an Edmund Burke or a Lord Chatham who had the capacity to personally define their rhetoric to the people in England at a moment in history. We now have the people of the United States being defined by fragmentary descriptions of what a people do. Rather than a single rhetor performing those constructions, we have instead what one might want to call a communication stage manager, like George Bush, who orchestrates fragments to which we should pay attention. He instructs us on how to put them together. If we follow his instructions, we are constructing the discourse which calls us into being. Horatio Alger pulled himself up by his own bootstraps to become a success. And in capitalistic America, in order to become a success in mobilizing collective power today, we must pull ourselves up by our own discourse.

We should not mourn the loss of "great speakers" — personal heroes, great men and great women that we should follow. If we can really come to appreciate the sense in which we are created by discourses, and come to honor discourse per se, as much for what it has done *for* us as what it does *to* us, we might have grown a lot; we might have changed a lot. Because if there is anything to this humanity as a collective thing, what's really humane about us is what we collectively have produced and reproduced in the form of discourse — what we continue to read, what we make our children read, what we make them listen to, what we say to one another. And if we can regard ourselves as being spoken by this discourse, created by this discourse, I think we are in a lot better position than the Germans were when they thought themselves fathered by their Führer. We have a more accurate understanding of what it means to be a human being and to understand where we came from.

The fragmentation does make it more difficult to hold somebody responsible for a state or condition that we disapprove of, but the fragmentation also makes it easier to have an authentic and understandable knowledge of where we come from, who we are, what we might hope to achieve. I could look at the fragmentation and throw up my hands as E. D. Hirsch did, and talk about what our poor kids don't know. What I hear is some expert saying that some group of people knows the wrong things. An expert is perfectly willing to run through an examination and say, "This is right, and this is wrong," but if the expert puts the moral twist on it, he or she is going to say, "Oh, my God. You are very ignorant; you are very stupid; you know the wrong things. You know all about television when you should know about books." This, to me, is arrogant and short-sighted. It doesn't leave "the people" or anyone else much room to grow or change.

When the child comes to my university class and says, "I can't read," or "I don't read well," or "I don't like reading," I'm not willing to say that this child is ignorant and needs to be reconditioned or reevaluated. I am much more interested in what people *do* know than what they *don't* know. I think we must concentrate on that in our new cultural situation. Yes, we are in a fragmented world. Yes, there are no sureties, no guarantees any more. Yes, the American character appears to be on the demise. Okay, all those things are true. But what *do* people know? What kind of lives are they creating? The world of fragmentation for me is a world of new possibilities, not necessarily a world to be afraid of.

In order to survive and get through the postmodern condition, rhetorical critics must learn that good criticism these days is good speechmaking. We are members of an audience and not imitators of the people who are on the platform or who are making the movies. As a result of this, our primary task in the postmodern condition, like the audience's, is text construction. We have to become very self-conscious about the sense in which we are in the process of criticizing and interpreting. Those words almost become inappropriate. In the process of criticizing and interpreting, we have to realize that we are making a speech, because every audience member is in that condition now. What confuses the matter is the ordinary or old meanings of the terms "to interpret" and "to criticize."

To interpret and to criticize used to mark one as being in the audience and relieved one of the responsibility of text construction. So we could be inarticulate if we were critics. We could be inartistic. We didn't have to be good dramatists if we were critics, because our job was to appreciate what was on the stage.

But in the postmodern condition, that's no longer the case. In order to be good critics now, we must be good speakers. And there's no way that we can write a good criticism without being perceived as having taken a politic position, having made moral judgments—all of the things that one thinks of as a part of a person who has a platform. Because we do have the platform.

Rhetorical critics can put fragments together in one of three genres or one of three forms of presentation. The form of one presentation would investigate the relationship between the sources of a text under criticism and what the text under criticism actually used from those sources—in other words, how the text we're looking at has pulverized or crushed or quarried the fragments that were available to it. The second possible structure would be to investigate how the text under investigation understood the fragments of society or the multiple audiences that were its targets—how the text constructed out of a multiplicity of audiences a sufficient vision of a homogenized audience that it could be addressed in one speech. The third possible structure to investigate an oration would be to look at the way the text under investigation was itself fragmented as it came to be a socially and culturally influential thing.

When we do criticism this way, our decision as to what documents we're going to focus on, what texts we're going to focus on, and what fragments of that text have been influential puts us in a frame of mind so that we're sensitive to that particular thing in our environment as it's developing. I could find an equal number of fragments at any moment I undertook a critical project. And I do it just like we teach students to give speeches. I get the thesis of my speech from what I judge to be the most influential or potentially influential fragments in a text I want to criticize. And then I do research just like we tell students to do it—not just simply at the library, but I attune my antenna to films and music and television and radio and newspapers and conversations around me, whatever comes before me while I'm doing this kind of an oratorical project. I'm in a sense single-minded. When I flip through the paper in the morning over coffee, after I've finished the sports page, I'm thumbing through parts of the paper I would never read if I weren't involved in this project. That's what I mean by "performative criticism." Criticism becomes a performance in the sense that oratory is a performance.

What authorizes any criticism is the wisdom of the fragments of the pieces that one puts together—what one chooses to put together, and whether or not it makes sense. Whether or not people can recognize it as something that for the moment for them is going to pass for the truth. And we have to put it together not just simply in terms of what makes sense for *us*. It's that second step that forces us to exercise judgment and reveals the degree of our wisdom. Who do we want to convince? And how does it make sense to *them*? Do other texts, other fragments, need to be added to make sense to them? Do we need to emphasize this text or to use less of it in order to make sense to them? Those adjustments are the adjustments that any rhetorician has made, whether trying to sell a car or arguing for the conviction of a criminal. It's exactly the judgment a rhetorician has to make. And it's that judgment that reveals his or her wisdom and the truth of what's being said. And we don't take things willy-nilly. We have something going for us.

One criticism of this position is that we lose all sense of scholarship, all sense of academic community. We become just preachers, because we make our own little criticisms like we're making a speech. How do we hold people accountable if we just select whatever we want to? Well, that's like suggesting that a rhetorician is unaccountable. And, Christ, we've spent our lives as rhetorical critics showing very specifically how every person who has the gall to address the public is made responsible by that public for his or her actions. Plato said it eons ago: Politicians have literally the least power in states where they do nothing which they will, only what they think best. They have to adapt to the audience. They have to control themselves. We as rhetorical critics are even worse than that. We not only have to adapt to our audiences, we have to be right.

One of the reasons we make this postmodern move is so that we will be able to say things differently than we ever could before. For instance, during the Enlightenment we learned that every social problem that we have is an effect of a cause. The causes of all social problems are beneath the surface, hidden somewhere in structures — in the way things are organized and put together, in the form of things.

Those of us on the left all want a revolution to come. And by "revolution" we mean a dramatic structural change in the way business is done. And I am just absolutely convinced that if we changed our economy from capitalist to socialist tomorrow, or if we changed the Soviet economy from socialist to capitalist, most of the social problems that bother us today would still bother us. The reason they would still bother us is because screwing around with the structure doesn't scratch the surface.

We can challenge the Enlightenment very directly, because it has given us our prejudice against the superficial. Back in ancient Greece, in the time when it was fashionable to construct speeches of praise and blame for historical and mythical figures in order to display the values of the culture, Gorgias of Leontini and Isocrates both constructed speeches in praise of Helen of Troy. And in both speeches, even though they were violently opposed to one another in terms of conflicting attitudes, theories of rhetoric, theories of politics, and everything else, both speeches held that the thing she most deserved praise for was her beauty in its purely superficial sense. It was something that was valuable for its own sake and not to be dismissed out of hand.

We've got a huge contradiction right now throughout our culture because we are conditioned, we are taught, to devalue the superficial, and yet in our daily lives the superficial probably exercises far more influence on us than we realize. Beauty is a fine example of that. The beautiful people are rich and powerful. Richness, power, and beauty go hand in hand with one another. And yet we think of beauty as something that is merely superficial. The real person is beneath the skin. We think of wealth as something that doesn't really matter. It's the spiritual source of the person that matters. All these are sources of ideology, and it's all part of the same bill of goods we were sold by the Enlightenment of trying to rationalize what ought to guide human community by constructing what does guide human community.

As a result of this, we tend to think of any solution as having necessarily to be a structural solution. To give a vivid contrast, Nancy Reagan comes out and says, "Just say no." This is a superficial, really a postmodern, response to the social problems of narcotics. And everybody ridicules her on the grounds that any acceptable solution to the problem of drugs has got to be more complex and complicated than that. It's got to be deep and structural. Yet that campaign is a very effective strategy in today's conditions.

We can apply this principle to the problem of racism. We originally approached the problem as a matter of structure—a matter actually of reconstituting the society (i.e., through the Thirteenth, Fourteenth, and Fifteenth Amendments to the U.S. Constitution). Every move we made with regard to racism for 125 years has involved some restructuring. We passed a law, established rules of evidence or rules of procedure in courts of law and elsewhere on how to enforce the law, amended the Constitution—and still racism is with us.

We are phrasing and posing social problems as if, naturally, they were the effect of deep structural causes. An example of this is the famous disease metaphor, where we say, "X is a problem. It's a disease." If we figure it as a disease and we use a medical metaphor, then that means that we're going to have to equate some social practice with a germ, a virus, or a disease. Go after it with medicine or surgery, and hope to cure it.

Now what does this do? With regard to a social problem like racism, it is suggesting that even in embracing a solution, the victims of bigotry must pay a higher price than the sociopathic bullies who offend them. Why? They have to wait. They have to wait to give the medicine time to work. So we can make some structural change here. We can pass the Civil Rights Act of 1964. This is supposed to stop black agitation. This is supposed to stop black outrage. Why? "Because we've responded to you. We have changed the structure. Give it time to work." The Civil Rights Act will work."

We're being told the same thing about the Thirteenth, Fourteenth, and Fifteenth Amendments: "Give it time. When the time is right, racism will disappear."

Another example of this is homelessness. We are so concerned with what causes people to be homeless, and what their motives are in being homeless, and whether or not we would be morally justified in helping these "lazy, no-good" people, that we forget to treat the symptoms. We forget to give them places to live.

A superficial analysis is actually, within our metaphors, a deeper analysis one that gets more to the real problem. A superficial analysis forces us to come to grips with what we want on the surface — what we want the end product to be. Structural analysis gets to be so complex and so devious in a sense that it leads us to believe that an intermediate goal is the real goal. It lets us jump up and down for joy when we achieve an intermediate goal.

Another example of this is my father's cancer. He had a particular lung cancer, and the doctor said that there was only one chance for cure. And the one hope for cure was that this tumor had not grown in such a way as to wrap itself around the aorta. There is in the medical community a big division between surgeons and nonsurgeons — those who like to cut and those who are reluctant to cut. Well, the surgeon's remedy is clearly a structural remedy — to get inside the body structure and to remove the cause, sort of like replacing a foundation that is full of termites. Because that was the hope for my father, the hope for a structural cure. My family was enthusiastic. We authorized the surgery immediately. I went right along with it. But later, we found out from my cousin who is a doctor that in eighty percent of the cases in this particular tumor, it is wrapped around the aorta. His one chance of a cure, and it was one chance in five of a successful cure by surgery.

The other option is to treat the cancer symptomatically. Treat the cancer's symptoms. Use radiation and chemotherapy to shrink the tumor and keep a watch on him. But now, as a result of having had the surgery, his life may actually have been shortened.

He had to go through this other treatment anyway because the surgery failed. But in the meantime he's flat on his ass for six months trying to recover from a chest cut that goes from his backbone to his sternum. And again, even when we know there is a structural cure, we never ask the question: Is the cure worth the price? Would it be better to treat the problem symptomatically than to try to treat it structurally? We have this initial impulse — I had it myself: If there's a possibility of a structural cure, go for it. We don't even think rationally about the superficial alternative. And that, to me, is an important critique of Enlightenment thinking.

I'm not saying that this is a panacea, that it's a cure-all, that there never is an occasion to fiddle with structure or to pass a new law. We can't look at a problem and say that it has no depth, or that depth doesn't matter. We don't want to repeat the error by saying that we want a shallow Gorgian sophistry, where we attend to nothing except the superficial. It is rather simply to call attention as a point of criticism to the fact that conceptions of Enlightenment rationalism have systematically devalued the surface and have never explored solutions of the surface.

From a postmodern view, we are forced to think of social problems superficially. Think about our use of the word "superficial." To be superficial is to be bad. You're not deep enough. But what happens if what it is you are dealing with is itself superficial? I am not going to get rid of skin cancer by removing my liver. I have to treat the surface of my body, because that's where the cancer is. The postmodern condition forces us to frame social problems superficially. Because if we're right in terms of the influence of hyperreal representation, any social problem will not be perceived as a problem until it is made hyperreal — that is, until it is recognized on the television sets and talked about. So, for instance, as long as we didn't talk about or publicize AIDS, it was a disease queers got. Once we started to talk about it, to publicize it, it became a social problem. It became a hyperreal social problem. It became more real than real. Why? Because people became afraid that if someone with AIDS touches you, you're going to be infected, for God's sake. So the stories they heard were blown up in their minds and so hyperbolized that the mediations of AIDS became more real than the disease itself.

When we are living in a condition like that, we are forced to frame social problems superficially. And this isn't bad. That's the mistake Eco and Baudrillard make: the notion that living in a hyperreal world creates worse living conditions for us. It doesn't. Because now I can work at the problem of bigotry and racism where it exists — on the surface of things, in representations that are made of other groups and our consequent representation of ourselves. The way we signify groups is our primary vehicle for representing ourselves.

Chapter Four

American Liberalism

The move in rhetoric and social theory in the twentieth century was really a move away from Aristotle and toward Kenneth Burke—a move away from a theory of rhetoric as a theory of persuasion, and toward rhetoric as a theory of identification. The two master terms are different in the work of these two theorists, but many rhetoricians didn't understand what we were doing. We knew Burke was important. We knew enough to read more Burke at least.

But we didn't understand the implications of Burke's work. At the time of Burke's speech to the Writer's Congress in 1937, all of his earlier radical books—*Attitudes toward History, Permanence and Change*—were already out. After the Writer's Congress, he wrote *Rhetoric of Motives, Grammar of Motives,* and *Rhetoric of Religion.* All three of them are almost studiedly liberal, conservatively liberal, in their political leanings. He attacked Karl Mannheim in ideology, and he attacked Marx's rhetoric of irony, and that was almost a moment of conversion for him. He knew that for the left it was a choice between being politically correct (a term that is being tossed about quite a bit these days) and being politically effective. Burke was with a group of relatively closed-minded Stalinists who wanted to be politically correct. And he said to them, "You're wrong. You need to be politically effective. Here's how you do it." But they did not do it. Burke was a more committed revolu-

91

tionary than the revolutionaries. When he presented the old left with an opportunity to do political good, realistically, rhetorically, and sensitively, in the United States — not to be politically correct, but to be politically effective — they rejected him outright. So he rejected them.

Burke knew that liberalism is all that will work politically in the United States. There's something very special about the fact that English is spoken in the United States. The history of England was odd, curious, eccentric, unlike the history of a lot of other places. And it created a culture, a lifestyle, a political system that were, and are in many ways still, unprecedented. It's copied all over the world now, and I think it is clearly the most successful organization for an industrial society. But liberalism doesn't have anything to do with economics. Liberalism is a matter of political relations among individuals in the state. It has nothing to do with economic arrangements within the state.

For me, a liberal is on the left of a relatively narrow spectrum of American politics. A liberal is, first of all, a firm believer in freedom of speech and exchange of information. The only free market I believe in is the free market of ideas, which to me is the heart of liberalism. Liberalism is also a political system that protects or insulates the people who live within it from the excesses of the power brokers. And it does this by persuading the power brokers that there are ways that they can't use their power, by carving out a space that we call in liberalism "privacy" — the rights of privacy. I am probably as much for the rights of privacy as the American Civil Liberties Union is for free speech. That, to me, is the heart and soul of liberalism. It is the political system that says, "There is some conceptual or literal space you can go where no one has the right to interfere with you."

I am committed to liberalism, and I've been worried for twenty years or more about how to theorize privacy with regard to some of the socialist arguments that I find quite compelling sometimes. I have difficulty understanding how we can discuss privacy without also tying that concept very closely to property. I'm not a free-market capitalist by any means, but I think that we need to have an ideological system in which the individual human organism has separateness, dignity, stature, visibility, and freedom — I sum that up as privacy. That's what I'm committed to; that's liberalism to me. I'm far more afraid of governments than I am of corporations. There have to be spaces where the body is free. One of the things that attracts me to some of the politics of environmentalism is this notion of places where bodies can go to be free. If my home is less free because I have to obey some patriarch, or if my property can be invaded, or if I don't have property, there are still places I can go where the body can be free. I can go to Yellowstone; I can go to Jackson Hole, Wyoming. That's attractive to me.

REMODELING LIBERALISM

This is more a confession of faith than it is an ability to demonstrate anything. But what I really believe we should be putting our energy into is remodeling liberalism. People get these hard-and-fast categories. They think of any ideology as a text already written. And it's not. It's a text that is in the process of being written. We *can* have effects on what the next generation is going to believe. If we didn't believe that, we would never have children. We can bring about change. We can affect the future.

Of course, there are certain things that we can't escape. Ideology is historically material. The kid you bring into the world is going to pick up liberalism everywhere he or she goes. There's going to be more reproduced than there is changed in any particular generation. But change is possible. It is far easier, far more comfortable, and far more humane for everybody involved to work change by remodeling liberalism than by bringing in a new system of government or a new ideological system. That's an enterprise fraught with terrible difficulty.

Some people are hunt-and-peck typists. I'm a hunt-and-peck theorist. I can pay attention to a problem now, today, but I have no idea how things fit together. I'm not suggesting that someone is going to write *the* book, or *the* final explanation for everything. I don't think that's ever going to happen. It may very well be that these little guerrilla forays into the rhetoric of liberalism are the way to go. I don't know; there might not be any other way possible. But there's a ton of work for ideologists to do right now by taking little parts of the ideology, like the concept "liberty," or the concept "morals" or "morality," or the concept "law," and talking about how they can be restructured. We have to find an ideological solution for ideological problems. We cannot solve an ideological problem by manipulating the infrastructure, manipulating the economy. We can't solve an ideological problem by creating a police state to insist on some kind of morality. It's got to be done term by term, argument by argument.

A left politics cannot be articulated globally. It cannot be articulated as a set of totalizations that apply to all states, nations, and cultures. It has to be adapted or translated into the particular culture and language that we are dealing with. We can have left politics in the United States, but we can't have a Marxist vocabulary in the United States. The Comintern International will not play in Peoria. All we're going to get at a Comintern International is a few disgruntled people, usually bourgeois, who are choosing the Communist Party or some other fellow-traveling pink attitude in order to distance themselves from the other groups that they think make them morally unacceptable because they are too bourgeois.

Marxism is about justice; it's about equality; it's about rational, realistic government and realistic policies. I've got to use the word "realistic." That's what it's all about. And we can have all of those things if it is culturally translated. What I'm suggesting is that if we're going to have a true politics of the left in Anglo-America, it must be liberal politics. There's no choice, because liberal politics is all that will fly here. If we cannot talk about what we want to accomplish in the terms of liberalism, then we are condemning ourselves to a life of marginality. This is what Burke is telling us.

The word *Marxissant* is a French word that frequently appears in new-wave discourse theories. I like the term because it's easy to say, and its English translation is terribly hard to say. Its translation would be "Marxist-izer." That "-izer" we put on the end of words means to treat something as if it were. For example, we might say, "Oh, he's a lawyer; he's just lawyerizing that." A Marxist-izer, a *Marxissant,* is one who accepts the fundamental categories and logic and maybe even methods of Marxist analysis, but is not a party member and is not committed to the social state or the dictatorship of the proletariat. A *Marxissant* believes that theory is alive, not frozen or sterile or orthodox, and it needs to be developed and moved forward. But most fundamentally Marxist-izers or *Marxissants* are more nationalist, in that they tend to deny the international aspects of Marxist theory. Marxist theory holds that if you are a worker living in Cleveland, you have more in common with a worker in Gorki than you do with a banker in Columbus. And this is not true. I don't mean "nationalism" in a chauvinistic or statist sense, but in a cultural sense. I almost never talk about "American this" or "English that." I use the phrase "Anglo-American," because the language that one speaks is the most important denominator of culture. We have more in common with people who speak our language than with people who don't.

"Nationalist" is the negative word that would be attached to Anglo-American culturalism. I don't approve of nationalism in a statist sense. But I do approve of it in a cultural sense. I don't mean it in terms of chauvinism, in terms of saying, "Anglo-Americans have it made, and we're the best in the world."

My overall political program is to find out the reasons for the failure of the American left and to make it more rhetorically effective. And what I see is that part of the failure of the American left has been the attitude that it has toward being politically effective—that unless we're out on the street promulgating a physical revolution with workers involved, we are somehow politically incorrect. In fact, all successful revolutions have been conducted by people who were fully integrated and involved in the political and economic structure of their day—not people who were alienated from it completely.

The alienated people are the cannon fodder of revolutions. That's a terribly elitist thing to say, but I believe it to be empirically correct. The one thing that we don't want is a left intelligent-

sia with a self-conception of themselves that their only moral imperative is to be cannon fodder. If that is the case, then we have
a leaderless left.

An academic operating in this political economy at this time
does the most good simply by filling the space that would otherwise be occupied by a fascist. The left academic, going through
the rituals, the processes of "publish or perish," is fulfilling those
obligations from a left political perspective rather than from the
perspective of the fascist who would be in that place if that person weren't.

The most mighty revolutionary act I ever did was not when
I told Hank Hawkins how to make a heat bomb. The most radical act I ever made was in 1980, when I de-gendered all of my
pronouns. Systematically, I say "he or she." It was the first time
in the lives of many of my graduate students that anyone had
ever done that. And I said that I would take points off papers
if I found any gendered stuff. And it stopped. When I started,
there was a generation of graduate students who resisted it, but
since 1983 or 1984 it has become the operating norm of the
department. And my colleagues have adopted it. It's as simple
as changing a pronoun. That can be an incredibly consequential political act.

As part of the left intelligentsia, we are acting out of a moral
obligation, often against our best interests. From my own sociopolitical circumstances, I have no complaints. I shouldn't be politically active. As a matter of fact, if you look at who I am — fat, old,
bald, middle-aged, living in Iowa, in a household with income in
excess of $80,000 — I ought to have voted for Bush and Reagan.
I mean, if it was a matter of self-interest, their policies make my
life more comfortable than the policies I would like to see in place.
As an intellectual whose political commitments are based on some
otherness, I'm always in the position of being an outsider. When
I talk about feminism, I'm a man. When I talk about blacks, I'm
white. When I talk about the working class, I'm a rich professor.

Why do I hold these politics against my apparent self-interest?
Because I think they are morally right. If I behaved only in a way
that was consistent with my social circumstances, I would be im-

moral. Further, I would be selling out the other groups. I flatter myself that the oppressed groups need me. In many ways, I'm the best they've got.

This rationalism simply acknowledges the fact that the peoples of the world are heterogenous and diverse, and that they are in a competition for resources—all resources. It has everything to do with politics, not with anything other than politics. Take an ordinary political competition in the United States: Democrats versus Republicans, or environmentalists versus industrialists. As much as we dislike the industrialists, we don't want to put them on Torquemada's rack. We may fantasize about dropping a nuclear bomb here or there, but we really wouldn't approve of that if someone did it. We probably don't really want to get much more violent than spiking a few trees in the Montana wilderness.

We certainly do not want environmental politics to destroy the economic infrastructure of the United States, because that would mean widespread unemployment, starvation, incredible problems. We want to forward our politics in such a way that we get what we want, or a measure of what we want, without doing violence to the economic infrastructure that lets us and our opposition coexist inside a statist structure.

Cultures work the same way. One world is fine. I'm all in favor of one world. But one world does not mean that the United States is not in competition with Japan. We are. We must compete. We don't want to destroy Japan. We don't want to drop a bomb on the Japanese any more. We don't want to do anything that harms their economic infrastructure. But neither can we permit them to do something that harms our economic infrastructure, because that literally means bread on the table and milk in the bottle for our babies. We must conduct ourselves politically with regard to other cultures in the world.

This is not to say that I am in favor of or would in any way authorize the unconscionable rape and pillage of Third World or Fourth World countries for their natural resources, any more than I would authorize that kind of behavior in a domestic political dispute between environmentalists and industrialists. Industrialists need to be caught up short by people who are relatively neutral in that controversy when they walk into a forest and literally cut down every living thing. Environmentalists need to be brought up short by neutrals or relative neutrals in that conflict when they are bombing lumber mills and threatening to put the economic infrastructure of the state of Washington out of business.

This sounds in some ways a lot like free-market capitalism, and I get very uncomfortable when someone from the radical right says something that I agree with. But, to me, it is a very rhetorical and a very realistic way of looking at the world. "We are all one" is a fine regulative ideal. But "we are all one" cannot be taken as a universal principle and still be political. We all want to be political. But frequently we don't recognize that there are times for us to be political in the interest of things that we do not wholly approve of.

Since we're at the point where we're getting really controversial in terms of politics, let's push this theory even further to the point where it gets really tight in the shorts. Compare Vietnam with Iraq. What should be a moral left posture with regard to the war in Iraq? There is a serious parallel between Saddam Hussein and Hitler. It's rhetorically excessive, yes. But the man did gas his own people. If he had been successful in what it looked like he was going to do, he would have controlled fifty percent of the world's oil reserves. The only thing the United States profited from in Indochina, the only thing of economic value in Indochina that the United States could not get cheaper elsewhere, was optical sand. That's it. That was the only conceivable economic interest there. So if we were wrong in opposing the Vietnam War, eyeglasses might have cost more.

The consequences of being wrong in opposing the Vietnam War were not horrible. However, if I am wrong in my opposition to the war in Iraq, the consequences are catastrophic: widespread unemployment, major depression. Again it is the materialist in me. I always think and talk about food on the table and milk for the babies. If the consequences get to be that dire, we have to back up. A pacifist on the left has to judge these two situations differently and probably has to agree with George Bush, even though that's a terribly uncomfortable position.

The important thing that the left has to do is to be America's conscience. The left has never really been in power, except for a few years when Franklin Roosevelt was President and Henry Wallace was Vice President. The left's strength has always been the fact that we conceive of things in moral terms. We want to take the right action. The difficulty with the left is that it has become in a sense too preoccupied with morality. Coming to the correct judgment, the one that we feel confident in, the one that we feel is right, is enough for us. That's why it is important for rhetoricians to theorize the left, because it's not just enough to be right, unless we win as well. In order for us to win, we have to engage in politics. And, as they say, we can't make an omelette without breaking eggs. We cannot achieve a political goal without compromises. We just can't do it. There is no such thing as uncompromised politics.

It requires relativizing, not compromising, moral stands. Relativizing them. The strength of the left's morality is based on a relativist attack on the absolute morality of the right on almost any issue that we can name. But once the left arrives at its own relativist judgment, it is treated absolutely. We could come up against the "Onward Christian Soldiers" bullshit from the right with the response, "I'm a pacifist. By God, I was out in the streets against the Vietnam War." We forget that we arrived at that position through relativist compromises and judgments. Once we are at that position, we say, "I'm a pacifist. Vietnam—never again." We treat it as absolute, as if it were scripture written in stone.

What this means is that, rhetorically, the left is incredibly inept and insensitive. Part of the left's problem is that any relativist is always at a disadvantage when arguing with an absolutist on any issue. The relativist always makes the mistake of accepting the other person's ground.

We have seen, for example, that the only alternative that the left has closely argued over the last 200 years is some form of state socialism, and this doesn't work. It simply is incapable of supplying demand. It would be, in my mind, an act of folly for us on the left to continue insisting that we imitate the Soviet Union at the very time that the Soviet Union has thrown up its hands at the failure of its sixty-year experiment. We're going to have to have some economic organization that looks more like it looks now than we would be very comfortable with. We have to get into the interior of business corporations. We have to fiddle around with their internal structure, with the way they think of themselves, with their motives. But I would not want this yet to be at the level of politics, because we don't have enough people who have thought carefully enough about the alternatives.

PROPERTY AND CAPITAL

We need to recoup property. One of the things I object to about socialist strategies is that they in effect object to all forms of property. If the Bolshevik experience in the Soviet Union teaches us nothing else, it is that collectivization is not a really good strategy. It is economic suicide over the long haul. There needs to be a genuinely liberal or left attitude toward property and property holding.

The left has virtually nothing to say about corporations, because the left has defined corporations out of existence. They say, "We don't need corporations. Corporations are the enemy. And property is the enemy. So we don't need to theorize that. It's just a big pie, and we'll just divide it equally." And equality becomes the big thing.

One of the problems is that socialism, particularly Marxism, doesn't work in a liberal state. It just doesn't work. No English-speaking country has ever voluntarily installed a communist or socialist regime, unless we call a labor party a socialist party. Of course a labor party has socialist leanings, but it is operated primarily within a liberal ideology. The reason is that the liberal ideology is very comfortable for people. It works.

I was listening to the free marketeers in Montana recently, and their most persuasive arguments had to do with the possession of property that was real property, where the possession of it obligated it or put a responsibility on the owner of the property in his or her own self-interest to do things to protect it and enhance it. But most of the people whose politics and power I object to only own property that is measured in numbers on a balance sheet and kept in a bank for them. It's not real property at all; it's just money.

Corporations are in fact committing murder. What else can we call the Bhopal accident? They could have done better, and they didn't. How do we hold Exxon responsible for the *Exxon Valdez* spill? And on and on and on.

There is a difference between capital and property. If I own a television set, I know that I am going to have to call a TV repairperson and keep it up. If I own a car, I'm going to have to change my oil and oil filter. If I don't do that, the thing's going to run down, and I'm going to have to buy a new car and it's going to cost me a lot of money, and I won't be able to use that money any other place. So I've got this built-in motive to take care of what's mine. If, however, I have, not a car, but the *cost* of a car sitting in the bank and drawing interest, my only motive is greed, not care. I'm making some money wherever my money is, unless I have it buried in the back yard. If I have it simply in an insured savings account at the bank, I'm drawing six, seven percent. If I invest it in the stock market, I might get it up to ten or fifteen percent.

As I make that money, I'm not really taking care of anything. I will create what Ernie Bormann would call "rhetorical visions of my golden years," and I'll have all sorts of capitalist aphorisms like "A penny saved is a penny earned," and "Save for a rainy day," and all that sort of thing. If we multiply this to the level of the advanced industrial capitalists—the three percent of the population that controls ninety percent of the wealth—we have the potential for the property's becoming simply a game. When I own a car, it's not a game. Since I'm an American and acculturated in America, my automobile is incredibly bound up with my understanding of liberty. If I can't crawl in a car and drive to California, I'm not free. So that car matters to me on an immediate and personal level. It's not a game.

My television set is not a game. If the surveys are right and I'm an average American, I spend a quarter of my life in front of this thing. I depend on it for my news. I depend on it for product alerts in terms of participating in the consumer economy. I depend on it for entertainment, companionship; I make it a babysitter for my kid. It just does a whole host of things for me. So it's not a game.

The wealthy capitalists, the advanced industrial capitalists, could make profitability into a game. How would they behave in this game? Well, I don't have to be really too prescient in terms of projecting this, because it's a fact. Capitalism in the '80s became a game in which the only motive for accumulating wealth was to keep score with regard to relative success in your life. As a matter of public policy or morality, there has been no motive for large capitalists to take care of property. Consider the people who are taking over airlines in a deregulated state. The number of airline accidents in deregulation has increased incredibly. In order to make a profit in that kind of a highly competitive industry, where do capitalists cut costs? They cut maintenance costs, and airplanes get less safe. Of course, they can't say that. They can't admit that that's the truth. But the FAA doesn't really have any way to check on it any more, since they don't have any required runs and that sort of thing. They simply have to make a profit because it's part of the game—to win.

Tobacco companies can insulate themselves from public policy and from the remaining vestige of morality which we have in America, which is usually confined to health issues, through diversification. My God, they own Nabisco. They own Planters Peanuts. It's an incredible building of horizontal corporations rather than vertical corporations. There's no longer an industrial organization or an industrial responsibility. According to free-market rhetoric, there needs to be competition or some semblance of competition for the system to work. Of course, we on the left have said that there has been only a semblance, a simulacrum, of competition for forty or fifty years. There's no real competition among the big three automakers. Now it's even easier for us to make a case. If I'm part of a holding company that has a major presence in five different industries, what does it matter to me if I'm losing ground competitively in industry number one, as long as I'm gaining in two, three, four, and five? As a matter of fact, under deregulation and the kind of breaks that the Bush and Reagan governments have given capitalists, there's a real motive for me to keep that losing industry, or that losing presence in the industry, because it becomes a tax write-off. Then I don't have to declare too many dividends for stockholders in my more profitable enterprises.

What we're talking about is property that is not cared about. It's capital. And so what I think we need to do in terms of responding to free-market rhetoric is to suggest that there's a distinction between capital and property—that those who manipulate capital, those who own capital, and those who own property behave in different ways in theory and in practice. Although free-market rhetoric is conceivably correct, there's a good point to be made with it only as long as we're talking about property. But it does not hold true if we're talking about capital. It's a matter of size. It's a matter of whether or not one is using one's money to buy more money, or whether one is using one's money to buy a piece of property in order to hold it and care for it.

Let's suppose that we put Yellowstone up for sale. Of course most of us think Yellowstone is priceless, and we can't really put a figure on it. But let us suppose that we are going to ask four billion dollars for Yellowstone. Who can afford it? The only people who can afford to buy Yellowstone are capitalists involved in some kind of a diversification procedure. The lumber industry isn't going to buy it. Weyerhauser doesn't have that much money. But once it's sold, Weyerhauser will no longer have to deal with the government or the Forest Service. They're going to have to deal with some person of the Donald Trump, T. Boone Pickens, or Frank Lorenzo sort. They will never be dealing with a property owner, because no property owner could muscle the capital necessary to purchase a national park.

If we draw a distinction between property and capital, the argument of the free market breaks down, or at least it can be countered effectively because it forces attention onto the behavior of corporate robber barons. It forces us to understand the be-havior of robber barons as robber barons, instead of as heroic figures of some sort.

The line between property and capital includes a number of things. Owner occupancy is one. This increases one's commit-ment to property. Permanence of possession is another. This too increases one's commitment to property. How willing would T. Boone Pickens be to buy Braniff Airlines if he knew that he would not be permitted to sell it for twenty-five years? I'm talk-ing about new ways of governing corporations. If we can push this argument far enough down inside corporations, free-market rhetoric will turn back on itself. A business corporation is not the local incorporated service station any more.

Union Carbide is so big that its administration is virtually equivalent to a government with regard to its employees and the property that it manages. It is virtually a government and not an owner. And free-market rhetoric suggests for us that when property is invested in a government, it loses. We all lose by it, because the government in New York or Washington or wher-ever the corporation is housed isn't on the scene. It's not there, or it's not physically in possession of the property that it's manag-ing. It's sort of like the relationship between the Bureau of Land Management and Yellowstone. The same thing prevails.

Capitalists talk about the corporations as fictional individu-als. They use body metaphors to describe the various functions. And they refer to the administration of the corporation organi-cally, very much as they might refer to the lobes of the brain. The corporate lawyer is the mouthpiece. The chief executive officer is the head of the corporation. They want to keep instan-tiating it in the person, the individual.

Just look at the words often used to describe individualism: "selfish," "greedy." Those are all terms derived from the fact that we've defined privacy and individualism in relation to property. You are an individual insofar as you have acquired the property that makes you a legitimate individual within property concep-tions of individualism and property conceptions of what private space is. To me, the most crucial problem is trying to figure a way to theorize privacy or the individual in such a way that it's not connected to property. The body works fine. But even with the body, an individualism of the body is not going to sit well with good thinking.

We've got to figure out a different form of economic organization that does not privilege a fictional individual. There's got to be a way to hold corporations responsible for criminal activity. And there's got to be a way to increase their respect for the property they own, let alone the property that other people own. Liberalism needs to develop a different way of theorizing the corporation in order to put the kind of responsibility on the people who are involved in corporate activities that liberalism traditionally places on the individual. The whole notion of the corporation as a fictional individual has gotten way out of hand.

There needs to be some place where we can hold corporations accountable for their actions. If a corporation commits murder, who do we put on trial? The right says, "Well, that's an insoluble problem. You can't do it. You can't put anybody on trial. So we won't have a trial. We just won't charge them with murder." The left pretty much acquiesced to that.

But the force of the law isn't enough to control corporations. It requires an ideological commitment, possibly through a constitutional amendment. Ideological commitments are stronger than law. It's harder to amend them, harder to revise them. If there is an inconsistency between a law and the Constitution, the law has to give, not the Constitution. And they are virtually all worded as regulative ideals, there's a lot of interpretive latitude with regard to what is guaranteed in the Constitution. We're talking at the level of ideology.

The Peabody Coal Company was a real famous rapist of the land, strip-mining in Kentucky. They would just leave something that looked like a moonscape. People got terribly upset with this and passed local and state laws that are actually tougher than federal laws in terms of land reclamation after strip-mining. Now if you drive down around the area where there's a lot of strip-mining in Kentucky, it's still ugly where the mining is actually going on, but they have almost as many people employed reclaiming the land.

A corporation like Peabody Coal that has to violate a law to make a profit employs lawyers for that very purpose. But it's one thing to be accused of criminal activity and stand to be fined $20,000 or whatever pittance it is that those laws require. It's quite another thing when your lawyer is involved in a federal constitutional battle, when you are violating the Constitution. Corporations that are held to be in violation of the Constitution almost rigidly snap to, like Marines coming to attention. They don't fight the Constitution.

Without this kind of ideological commitment, capitalists will continue to play the game to win at whatever costs. Gordon Gekko, in the film *Wall Street*, is a caricature of an American capitalist. Is he a hero or a villain? This isn't at all clear. Gekko's a man of action. Gekko has a way of getting what he wants. He rewards his followers. He doesn't break any laws that everybody else doesn't break in his business. For him, the limit of his activity is no longer morality; it's the law. And this is the primary symptom of the decline into decadence. The cause of it may be Watergate. In the '70s, the "smoking gun" rhetoric was an exclusively Republican rhetoric, though it isn't any more. "I wasn't the first to do it, and until you can show me in a court of law incontrovertible proof that I did it . . . " and so on. We used to hold every American citizen, from Presidents and corporation presidents down to red-dirt tobacco farmers, responsible for a code of conduct that exceeds the expectations of the law. But now the bound of the law is the bound of morality, except for those in the religious right, in which case morality knows no bounds.

LAW, MORALITY, AND LIBERTY

We've got three entities: "the law," "morality," and "liberty." Morality is the space *between* liberty and law that establishes a bound or code of conduct that exceeds the requirements of the law, to which people in a free society voluntarily consent. They consent not because they're forced to or because they endure social pressure if they don't, but because it's right.

Liberty has nothing much to do with morality. Liberty is a very selfish kind of thing, whereas morality is ultimately a very giving and nurturing kind of thing. We can test this simply by reflecting on mothering. When we are being most nurturing of our children, we are most approximating the behavior of a tyrant. And if we think of the ways in which our mothers have annoyed us in the past, it has always been when they have put some restriction on our freedom or our liberty in the name of our own good. So the move for morality is sort of a mother right. We learn morality primarily from our nurturers, and society is structured in such a way that our nurturers are almost always our mothers. Morality, therefore, tends to get a peculiarly and often exclusively feminine cast. We went through a period in the nineteenth century of about sixty years when we were absolutely convinced that women were the custodians of morals. There was one standard of conduct when in the presence of a lady, and another standard of conduct in the presence of the guys. And that still hangs on to a certain extent.

But morality is tyrannical. Morality in a sense is almost anti-"free." Morality and liberty mix and mix well, but they mix well only when there is some give on both sides. The free person must acknowledge bounds, limits, on his or her own conduct. Nothing in liberty forces that, and if the state forces us to do that, we don't have liberty any more. So it's got to come from within. It's got to be our choice to do this. That's why it's so shocking and so disturbing when we see the law become the bound of morality. This falls under the heading of what I want Raymie McKerrow to mean when he says "critique of freedom." A critique of freedom asks, "Are you using your freedom wisely? Are you using it properly?" And if you are living in a community where the bounds of morality are equal to the bounds of the law, you have misused your liberty. I can't force you or persuade you to do anything differently; I can just simply tell you that you are not using your liberty wisely when you do not acknowledge that there are moral bounds over and above liberty.

From the morality side, there has to be at least pluralistic tolerance, and maybe something even stronger than that. Morality has to be kept a matter of personhood, such that if I disapprove of any conduct that you're engaged in, I can say that I disapprove of what you're engaged in, but there will be no relationship of power involved in this. I will not try to cut you off from your family inheritance. I will not fire you. I will not complain about you to the police. I will simply make a moral claim on you and leave it to you to act.

This is why I reject the morality of the radical right. The radical right is convinced that they have a road map to truth and virtue in the holy scripture, and they believe that they know what morality is, and they are willing to impose this on other people. The question of abortion, for example, is a very tricky question. We're never going to resolve it in terms of the rights of the fetus and the rights of the mother. We're never really going to resolve that in liberalism. But the question is, should anyone be burning down an abortion clinic? Should anyone be marching or parading in front of an abortion clinic? Should anyone be agitating to get the state to intervene with repressive-state apparatus, some kind of police power, to force clinics not to perform abortions? That's when morality is exceeding its bounds. Morality should not be constructing laws, and that's exactly what the radical right is trying to do. It is cooperating in this tendency to make the bounds of morality equal to the bounds of the law. In a good liberal civil society there is a space between the morality and the law, and that space between morality and the law is what allows liberty to exist. If morality coexists with the law, none of us is free.

If we live in a society where everyone is free, then we have to establish rules about just how far those liberties go. And the liberty can go no further than the space. If it belongs to everybody, then nobody has rights there to the exclusion of anyone else.

There needs to be at least a regulative ideal of what freedom is. That may be what environmental rhetoric can construct for us. If we translate keeping a public park into moral terms and take it away from liberty, then we are going to be tyrants. We are going to run afoul of this free-market rhetoric and be virtually unable to defend ourselves if we make it into a moral issue. If we make it into a political issue, we're probably going to win, but we're going to trivialize our accomplishment. We're not really going to solve what we want to solve. We're still going to have the conflict of interest between the spotted owl and milk on the lumberjack's table. We must take what, for me, is the high road by doing a remodeling job on liberal ideology and talking about the space of liberty, so that whatever is done by individuals in a national park or a national forest is done with respect.

MULTICULTURALISM

One of the issues that liberals in America must confront is the heterogeneity of our society. To talk about ethnic differences, we are talking about essentially semiotic differences. We are talking about signs that are socially constructed that say, "This practice makes me Italian or Jewish," "This practice makes me Nigerian," "This practice makes me Brazilian." These are signs that we identify with cultures.

When the Congress on Racial Equality (CORE) was formed, the civil rights movement was still basking in the togetherness mood of Martin Luther King. The political object of CORE was to make the color of the skin no more significant in human interactions than the color of one's eyes. This was a very powerful metaphor for me, because although we may pay attention to whether somebody has blue eyes or brown eyes because they are particularly attractive, or set well, or mix well with the complexion, it doesn't make any difference to us. The goal of the civil rights movement was to make the complexion that same sort of invisible personal feature. But the blacks in CORE got very offended because there were so many whites involved in it. The feeling was one of "black power" before Stokely Carmichael. It was a feeling of nationalism and ethnicity that was raised up, and it changed the entire character and direction and nature of the civil rights movement. It shifted it from a fundamentally integrative move-ment, designed to do what I regard as really productive social surgery, and transformed it into a kind of movement that I have been very suspicious of. The insistence of maintaining this mark-er of separateness, a difference that makes a difference, does noth-ing except reproduce the conditions that keep racism coming back generation after generation after generation.

Sometimes I think I must be terribly conservative in some of my readings of multiculturalism. If I get up on the right side of the bed in the morning, I worry about multiculturalism. If I get up on the left side, I don't. Markers of difference in social formations are always potentials for oppressing that which is marked out.

Integration used to be a real powerful ideograph. It's not much any more, because when whites say "assimilation," what we really mean is assimilating blacks into white culture, rather than whites into black culture. I guess that if I had to say what I be-lieve about racism, integration is what I believe. It goes both ways. Eddie Murphy is not a millionaire because blacks watch him. He has a huge white audience. Jazz is an art form that originated in a black community, but it isn't black any more. I've seen some white rappers on TV recently. So the culture flows both ways. Integration or assimilation flows both ways. But at stake are two things that the human groups have great difficulty giving up: their identity as white or their identity as black; their identity as male or their identity as female. And all of the markers that go with race or gender.

I've had moments when I have taken great pride in my eth-nic and cultural her tages and origins, and I can appreciate other people doing the same. But I had a real good friend in Mem-phis, a singer who made it big. I would never furnish my house the way he furnished his house. Everywhere he went he wore chains. Fifty thousand gold chains. Zebra skins on the wall. He had an employee, a barber, whose only job was to shave his head every morning, so that he would stay bald. He wore shades and his dashiki, always open to reveal his hairy chest and his chains. I wouldn't dress like that or appoint my house like that, but it has no bearing on blackness making a difference. That's simply a matter of style. I could find whites with outrageous taste that I'd never decorate my house like, too.

But we should regard that as a matter of taste, and if the ethnicity manifests itself in that way, then that's fine. But if it achieves status as an independent political symbol, it's fundamentally divisive. It's reproducing the conditions of oppression. But now most politics today that involve groups of people are in fact divided along those ethnic group lines: the Chicano community; the feminist drive for separation, particularly among lesbian feminists; the very powerful rhetoric of a Spike Lee that identifies even more the ethnicity of the black community. I think it's very dangerous.

On the other hand, in terms of building the economic position and the political position of the community involved, there's no question that it works. I don't live in fear, but I greatly fear the possibility of a Hitler. America is not that different from Weimar Germany in many ways. The anti-Semitism of Weimar Germany was encouraged not just by white Christian Germans, but also by Jewish Germans. So for a while they were forced to live in a ghetto, but they continued to live in a ghetto when they were no longer forced to. They opposed intermarriage as much as the dominant group opposed intermarriage. If we have a state that is based on three or four sovereignties, the potential for conflict is always there.

When I get up on the right side of the bed, I read Malcolm X as dangerous or threatening. When I get up on the left side of the bed, I think he's great. I'm really ambivalent about this. But I don't think there's a problem with integration, frankly. That is why I always come down on the side of integration. Because what you have to lose is a praxis that is always already dead. If you are here rather than Italy or Africa, it's because you left Italy or Africa. Your ethnic roots are there, and that's fine, but it's a dead praxis; this is a new praxis. I would say that also holds true for blacks whose ancestors were brought here against their will, because they were born here. This is the only praxis they've ever known.

We had a delegation from Nigeria tour the communication

building at Memphis State one year when I worked there. They were being chauffeured around by David Assie, who was very active in the Carmichael faction. And he was just glorying, eating up the fact that he was showing around his African brothers. They were all state officials and given a lot of deference. When he brought them for a tour of our communication building as a model facility, I was introduced to them. And one of them pulled me aside. He was the assistant minister of information, or something like that, in Nigeria, and he said, "I'm having a real problem with your guide. He keeps talking about finding identity. What does he mean?"

SOVEREIGNTY AND SOLIDARITY

One can think about power in two general categories very productively. One can think of power as fitting into the category of "sovereignty" or as fitting into the category of "solidarity." And what I mean by "sovereignty" is someone using the power of the bayonet on some right that they claim in order to enforce a particular set of laws—to force a community on folks. "Solidarity," on the other hand, is a feminine power. It is the power that is based on Jewish-mama guilt. It is a power that is in a sense interior to a human being. It is based upon your plea to me, not threatening me with anything that you might do, but threatening me with my opinion of myself, as it were—placing a claim on me, so that your power claim on me is like a Jewish mama saying, "Oh don't worry about me, I'll just sit in the dark alone this Sunday evening." This is a power claim, and there's no mistaking the fact that it's a power claim. But it's a power claim that's based on the guilt factor. It's generated from within me rather than from without.

The rise of Christianity was a revolution; there's no other way to think about it. It was the first revolution. It captured an empire; it transformed an empire. The Christian revolution was successful because at that time in the development of societies, people did not understand that a successful state must be held together by both sovereignty and solidarity. The Roman Empire had sovereignty. It established sovereignty over multicultured peoples and brought them together in the same state, and they were held together by the point of a sword. The genius of the Roman Empire—why it was allowed to operate so long—was the way it set up sovereign governments. As long as the people in an area that the Romans had conquered paid their taxes, Rome did not interfere with religion, school systems, or festival days. All of the things that made for the cultural solidarity of that people were kept intact. And all Rome demanded from them was their sovereignty. So you had pockets of strong cultural solidarity, like in Judea. In effect, they were still an independent people. There was no Romanizing going on among the Jews because of the power of their religion and their customs and traditions—the solidarity of the community.

From my point of view, when the Jews decided to defend themselves politically from the Romans by exporting Christianity, they made an absolutely brilliant move. They played upon the lack of cultural solidarity in Rome. And they simply said, "You do not have cultural solidarity in your Empire and we can provide it." And ultimately the Christian revolution succeeded.

The American system of government operates primarily because it exercises sovereignty in such a way as to encourage solidarity. That is not to say that solidarity always emerges or that we never rely on the point of a bayonet, but rather that we use sovereignty in such a way as to encourage cultural solidarity. That's also why postmodernism is such a tremendous threat to the U.S. form of government, because multiculturalism and the fragmentation of American culture claim that the solidarity allegedly produced by the exercise of American sovereignty no longer exists.

The groundswell of patriotism that occurred during the Persian Gulf War is an example of solidarity. The left has nothing to fear from an expression of solidarity in the wake of Desert Storm. The question is, what is being unified in solidarity? We have reached a point of social organization where we can no longer demand of solidarity that it be a solidarity of individuals.

We are now to the point where we have to think about solidarity of cultural formations—in other words, how do groups hang together rather than how do people hang together?

This is not a dramatic change in liberalism's way of doing business. It just asks us to be a little bit more abstract and a little bit more complex in our thinking, so that we now have to figure out ways in which African-Americans, Asian-Americans, Irish-Americans, as groups, have conditions of solidarity among them —rather than saying that these people of African, Asian, or Irish descent form a solid group because they're Americans. So we're looking at the conditions of coalition, rather than assuming that there is a native American intelligence or an American identity. We're assuming instead that there are indeed multiple racial, ethnic, and gender identities, and that the job is to construct a society in which all of these different identities are compatible. They don't necessarily have to be swapping spit. But they have to be compatible.

I'd like to see cultural solidarity; I'd like to see us be able to totalize multicultural fractions. But in the past we assumed the unity of all Americans and therefore inferred that if someone expressed an interest that was different from what we thought was genuinely American, they were somehow traitorous, criminal, or treasonous in some way. And we had to come down on them with the force of law. What's evil is the assumption that the solidarity comes first, that it's the natural order of things. But the fragments come first, not the solidarity, and the solidarity is not eternal.

Chapter Five

The People

I was educated that the great controversy about Kenneth Burke
was whether or not he was a unique force unto himself or an
Aristotelian. Marie Hochmuth Nichols, one of the old buffaloes
in our field, was arguing that he was an Aristotelian. The *raison
d'être* of our field was speech criticism, and people were so used
to neo-Aristotelian criticism that they were unable to escape it
and try something new. They were looking for another formula
with which to criticize speeches, and all they got from Burke was
the pentad: actor, scene, act, agency, purpose.

I found, in an obscure little place, a speech that Kenneth
Burke had given to the 1937 Writer's Congress, which had been
published in a book that had been out of print since 1940. The
essay had never been reprinted. The reason it had never been
reprinted was that the Writer's Congress was part of the Red Front
in the '30s, and during the McCarthy period we didn't want to
embarrass Kenneth Burke by reminding each other that he had
a Stalinist background. In this speech Burke was making the argument that the position of the Communist Party could not be
presented in America in its current rhetoric. It had to be coded
in the terms of America so that the message could get out through
a rhetoric of populism. The key term to argue for, Burke said,
was the term "people."

A few years before finding this speech, I had published a

piece called "In Search of 'the People' " in a national journal. It was a real creative effort for me. It was a discovery. It was a mining, if you will, of the speeches of Edmund Burke in order to come up with something that made sense to me. And what made sense to me was an understanding of the way in which a people is formed.

Any government has, as a part of its state papers, the argument that what in some way authorizes the acts of power of that government is the consent of the governed. It may use a phrase like "we the people of the United States" in American state papers. And what this suggests is that there is an entity out there in the social world—some place where all individuals come together with a like mind, a shared subjectivity—that they can safely be designated by the collective noun that refers to them all, "the people." My claim is that this term "people" is a rhetorical device. It is intended to take a collection of individuals who really don't have that much in common, and to get them to behave as if they were a single entity by describing for them in praiseworthy tones what "a people" is and does.

As citizens of the United States, it is our moral obligation to play the part of "we the people of the United States" when serving on a jury. We must not be biased. We must get rid of our personal opinions. We must let ourselves make a decision and judgment on the basis of the evidence created and render an objective and honest verdict in the name of "the people." It is a seductive device that gets us to give up our own individuality for the collective good. A court of law has always been my favorite example of this. Even the arrangement of the furniture is designed to get us to give up control of our individuality and surrender to the collective. There are hard wooden benches to sit on where we can't possibly be comfortable. We are in the presence of a person who wears a black robe and is flanked by the flag of the United States and the flag of whatever state it is we are operating in, sitting on a raised platform behind a huge bench so that we couldn't tell if there were anything ordinarily human about the man or woman at all. There is a bar separating the audience from the participants in this trial and another bar separating the jury from the attorneys and the judge.

We can see only an impression of power, and then of course if we are going to testify, or if we are going to serve on a jury, we have to take an oath; whether we are Christians or not, we swear on the Bible. The very ceremony of oath taking constitutes a real coercion of our interests. All of these are devices for getting us to surrender our subjectivity and to participate in a rhetorically created collective subjectivity.

This is very similar to my theory of "the people," and it is an issue in mass communication as well. I have a great deal of respect for Dallas Smythe, a Canadian theorist of mass communication, who suggested that thinking of television programming as we would think of a play, for example, is wrong. We tend to think of television only as entertainment, and we think of the show that is put on television as having a relatively exclusive relationship with the people who are watching it. The purpose, we believe, is to increase their enjoyment, to increase their pleasure in some way, as a play might increase one's pleasure. But the situation is different with television. When we are dealing with drama, "the play's the thing," in Shakespeare's words. The play is not the thing in television. The thing in television is to attract large numbers of viewers, so the television show is really more like a fishing lure than it is like a play. It's not so much intended to pleasure us, except insofar as we approach pleasure and avoid pain. The main thing is to get us to attend to it.

Once we are members of the audience, what the television moguls do is sell us as a commodity. The purpose of television is to attract audiences, which are then sold to advertisers, and that's how the moguls make their money. This makes imminent sense. This is one theory that is so sensible that I think it is clearly the way things operate in the industry, and even mainstream number crunchers would pretty generally agree with Smythe's portrayal of what television entertainment programming is all about.

The television audience is in a position of being spectators, but not a "people." A spectator is importantly not an actor. The subject position of the spectator takes very few risks. The subject position of the spectator takes no oath. The only people in a courtroom who have never taken an oath are the people who are just there to observe it. The television audience does not promise in any way to give up control of their own subjectivity for the interests of the larger group; there is no self-sacrifice in their behavior. They naively approach a television program at least as a pastime — a noise in an otherwise empty world for them. Perhaps they approach it, God help them, for pure pleasure and pure entertainment. But all of these are self-aggrandizing motives that do not call for self-sacrifice. And it seems to me that when we are talking about mass communication in television, the audiences that are attracted and then sold are never involved actors in a way that "the people" are.

SPECTATORSHIP

In the late '40s and the early '50s, television was sold to us as "our window on the world." It was going to expand our horizons and expand what we knew and our capacity to act in the world. We did not think about the true nature of being spectators, however. When we talk about something being our "window on the world," think of the metaphor: "window on the world." We are there at the window; we can open it; we can shout out through it. But the television set is not a window. It doesn't allow us access to the world we are observing. It only allows us to see a representation of the world, because we can't inject ourselves into the action, literally, of what we are observing. Any impulse we have to action is sublimated. All of these public education campaigns that we see are, in my view, bound to fail, if only because they are public *education* campaigns, not public *action* campaigns. The more we try to educate people about the issues of the environment through television, the more they are going to take it for granted that somebody is taking care of this problem and they don't need to do shit about it.

Contrast the education campaigns of the environmentalists with the education campaigns we have had for dealing with AIDS. The bottom line of the education campaign with AIDS has always been that you can get this disease and it is incurable. Therefore, by virtue of being human and sexually active, I am at risk, and action that I take ordinarily on an everyday basis puts me at risk and inevitably involves me in what's going on. There we have a true example of education's informing action where action is unavoidable. If I am talking about people in owl suits in the lumber country, or I am talking about the *Exxon Valdez* here in the middle of Iowa, I am not forced to act in those regards. I do not ordinarily act in those regards, so any information that I learn about it is like a thrilling story from the *Arabian Nights*. It is something I have fun with, believing it or not. It may shape my political consciousness. It may make me more liberal if I am liberal, more conservative if I am conservative. It may provide a romantic flare or an anecdote that helps me operationalize my politics in one way or another. But it is not going to constitute my politics like AIDS will.

The educational process can require involvement. My students are never in a spectator position. I don't permit them to stay in a spectator position. In other words, when I am involved in a teaching situation, my students will act in terms of their conversations with me. They will engage in speech action with their egos, if not their identities, on the line. Those of us who write for journals are acting in the same way. We are going public. We are at least taking some of the anxiety risks of the public speaker by going public with what we say and finalizing and sealing it into print. So there is a speech action or a writing action that is being engaged in.

Notice how different this is from television, where we are in a spectator position. There is no supposition whatsoever about what we will be like when watching any particular TV show. The television moguls don't know or care whether we are fully dressed or in our underwear, whether we talk back or sit silently, whether we nod in agreement or redden in anger. All they care about is that *we are there,* so that the conditions of spectatorship and the motives of spectatorship are totally undefined by the object that we are spectating upon. There is no risk because there is no necessity of action. Now I'm not suggesting that people cannot or will not take a story on the *Exxon Valdez* as a cue for action. There is always going to be a reading minority out there who get enraged and will use their window on the world *as* a window on the world, but this is not going to be the ordinary and usual response. There is nothing about the communication situation itself that inclines people to act. Thinking is acting, saying is acting, only when we make it so — only in a situation when we are forced to think, to act, and when we put ourselves on the table, where we risk something in thinking and acting.

However, if we consider news coverage of the Persian Gulf War, many analyses suggested that the news of the Persian Gulf was ordinary television programming — that, as is typical, the audience were mere spectators. They were treating the producers of that news, the people who were broadcasting the news, as manipulating an audience in an everyday, business sort of way. But when a war happens, we don't have the 5:00 news; we have round-the-clock news. We have people who were so addicted to watching CNN in this war that they went to sleep at night with the television on and were sleeping so lightly that they could be awakened from their nightly sleep at 3:00 in the morning by news breaking in the Middle East over the television set that they had left on all night. This is not ordinary behavior.

In a time of crisis like a war, like the Persian Gulf War, people who are observing television are not just spectators. They are participants. They are there. The war is quite obviously being conducted in their collective name. Over and over and over again, we heard that "our men and women" in the Persian Gulf were there "for us." They were there representing us. They were our people in the Middle East. This is a political collectivization. It is an instance of using a channel of mass communication for political purposes.

Too many people make the error of genre-izing television. When we talk about a channel of communication, we are talking about something that is fundamentally content-neutral, like my coffee cup here. We call it a coffee cup because I can pour coffee in it, and I can drink coffee from it, but sugar could fit in there as well as coffee or tea. Certainly, if there were nothing in it, it would still be filled with air, another substance. Lots of things could fill it. We have a notion of communication as operating over channels. Whatever else we may be distorting, one thing we are getting perfectly clear is that television is a channel of communication, and a number of things can move through and across it.

When we are talking about a business-as-usual perspective on the news, it's safe to talk about the news primarily as spectator-inspired entertainment. But it is possible to use this medium of communication, this channel of communication, for other purposes. It's possible to create a "people" by using television as a channel. We can't do it every day, not because of any limitation of the medium, but because of the limitation upon the individuals watching it. If we remember the sense of hysterical preoccupation that each of us had in the first eight to ten days of the Gulf War, that spirit of hysterical preoccupation is incredibly difficult for a sane person to maintain. If we acted and behaved this way for a long period of time, they would come with white suits to lock us in a rubber room, literally. We just can't stand the intensity that is involved in contributing our little bit to collective power. We have to fade back for a while. We have to relax. We have to give it up. We have to let even something as momentous as the Persian Gulf War become for us matter-of-fact, everyday business. It has to become an everyday part of our lives. If it doesn't become an everyday part of our lives that we anticipate and expect, we will go nuts.

COLLECTIVITY

So we are not going to find the use of television as a collectivization medium on a daily basis, as a rule — only in a time of crisis. When the President of the United States is about to be impeached, when a crisis like Watergate occurs, when we are on the verge of a war, or when we have odd and ironic things like Vietnam War protests or a *Challenger* disaster, we will then have the capacity of the media to collectivize. At that point it is proper to talk about "people," but it is a grave error to look at rhetoric, any rhetoric, in a crisis and see it as ordinary and mundane and in the familiar genres of the everyday, because crisis is not an everyday event. A crisis is extraordinary, and we have particular kinds of rhetorical and discursive responses to a crisis that make any medium of communication distort it, transform it, and appropriate it in the public interest. In a time of crisis, this is absolutely essential in order to provide collective force.

The political collectivization process is marked by its insistence upon self-sacrifice as a moral obligation: "You must not ask what your country can do for you, but what you can do for your country." So that the same spirit of the Peace Corps, the spirit of self-sacrifice, is the spirit that motivates the political concession of people. It is noticeably absent in television audiences. I don't think we need a theory of "the people" to explain television audiences. What we need is a theory of "spectatorship" or a theory of "the public," which is of a wholly different order.

The whole notion of "public" is a Latin notion, a Roman notion. And there is a sense in which early twentieth-century thinkers such as Dewey, and even today such people as Habermas, are a little bit confused by what they mean by "public." They seem to think of it as a place or a site, as one interpretation of the term. And another equally wrong interpretation of the term "public" is as an animate notion, a synonym for "people," as one would say, "The public expects or believes this or that."

The notion that "public" is a space or a place, a site of some sort, is probably the most defensible traditional conception of it as far as I am concerned. When one is in one's own sphere, behind the walls of one's own manor, safely within the confines of one's own institution—be it monastery or corporation or academy or university—one is not *in public*. So in this phrase, "public" has a kind of floating signification. Basically, we are not in public when we are in a place where we are comfortable—where we feel that we could let our hair down, and we are not taking very many risks.

Therefore, the notion of "public" changes because any time we enter a particular institution for the first time, we are not usually comfortable. Most people wouldn't be; we are fish out of water.

We have to learn a new way to talk, a new way to think, a new way to act. After we have been there a while, it becomes far more comfortable for us.

Being in public has a great deal to do with this notion of risk. "Public" is a site, or a place, where people take risks in doing what comes naturally to them and behaving as individuals and being eccentric. What we recognize as "publicly acceptable" behavior includes rules like "Don't use four-letter words," "Cover your body," "Don't belch," "Don't put linguini in your milk." All of these are rules that people set up in order to protect or insulate themselves. If we behave in this way, if we speak in this way, if we conduct ourselves this way, we won't call attention to ourselves, and the danger-producing elements of the environment will not attract us. Civilized behavior is in many ways like insect repellent. It's something that we put on in order to keep the dangers of social life away from us when we are in those places.

This notion of "public" as equivalent to a site or a place depends entirely on our capacity to think of its dialectical negation, or the "private." It is really this silent term, "privacy," that we are theorizing—not "public" at all, but "privacy." In Dewey's world, the private is the given, the understood. For Dewey, the private is natural and understood and obvious, and so what he really means to discuss is the public, and he discusses the public as a dialectical negation of the private without ever mentioning the private. He lived in a society that valorized and glorified the private, made it seem hegemonically natural. Private property, private enterprise, private home, freedom from search and seizure, "The government can't interfere," "A man's home is his castle," and all of those other signs that we have that designate the private. Fundamentally, John Dewey says nothing more than that the public is what's not private, and yet he never discusses what privacy is and what the conditions of privacy are.

The same is true with a lot of the early sociologists and social theorists. It was so obvious to everybody that "all men are created equal" and that we are individuals that they never bothered to theorize the subject. One would have to be a weird Austrian psychologist like Freud to think about the necessity of theorizing subjectivity at all, and when we do theorize subjectivity, most of the people in the world will think how impractical we are because of how obvious it is that human beings are individuals—how obvious it is that we are private organisms. Sociologists had the same trouble in theorizing society as in theorizing people, because they were saying that society is what individuals are not.

The other usage of "public" is as a human being. This is where one takes "public" as a separate designator for what I've called "the people." A lot of people have asked me, "Do you own the word 'people,' McGee? Isn't this just a synonym for 'public'? Don't people say, 'The public believes this' and 'The public believes that'?" I say, "No." The concept of "people" is constitutively written into the political structure of every nation in the world, I believe. I don't know of the Eastern nations; I'm not positive about China. I am about Japan. But certainly of all the European nations, the Soviet Union, the United States, this notion of "people" is an operating part of the rhetoric that constitutes the state. We don't talk about "the public"; we talk about the consent of "the people." The difference between "people" and "public" is a normative one.

The people in most constituted discourse is a sovereign power. The people are powerful. They are "aweful," full of awe, awe-inspiring. They are terrifying in the extreme. The people have the capacity to intimidate tyrants. This is the origin of liberal theory, the origin of Mao tse-Tung's communism when he talks about the journey of the 1,000 steps or the 1,000 days, the origin of Lenin's belief in the ultimate victory of Soviet communism—the power of the people and their ability to terrorize.

I think about this when I go to a football game. Most of us cannot begin to imagine what being in the presence of 250 million people in the same space would be. I go to a football game, and there are 70,000–80,000 people all together at once, and, boy, I get claustrophobia sometimes. I mean, there are just too many people there. And they scare the hell out of me. I see them drinking at a football game, and I get scared because they do irrational things. They pick people up and pass them up the rows.

Individuals all have rule-governed, behaviorally acquired conditions and controls over what they do, and for some reason in groups these disappear. The meekest, the mildest, the calmest people — 200 of them together become suddenly vocal, aggressive, militant, and frightening. One little old lady with blue hair and tennis shoes is not going to scare anybody, but you get 150 of them in front of an abortion clinic talking about saving the world for Christ, and they are scary. The essence of collectivity is to create power. It's a hard power to describe. That's why we have so many words like "the masses." Does it mean anything? Or "the people," which is an equally empty and meaningless phrase. There are words that we create in an attempt to describe an indescribable kind of power — the power of a collectivity, of ungoverned, undisciplined human beings whose behavior is totally variable in every direction and hence unpredictable. We can shoot at them, and we don't know whether they will run away or tear us limb from limb. We can talk to them, and we don't know whether they are going to cheer us or tear us limb from limb. It's like the drunks in the end zone of the football field. They could all of a sudden grab some poor woman from the front row and pass her up to the back row — no sense to it at all, no sense at all.

"The people" are irrational, and it's important that they be irrational. We can't control or influence the behavior of a tyrant unless we, "the people," are truly awe-inspiring. A tyrant with all the devices of police forces and the military at hand is not going to be afraid of anything that he or she can predict. But what scares tyrants is specifically the people's capacity, because of their numbers, and their irrationality — the fact that their behavior is unpredictable and hence virtually uninfluenceable. This is what democratic theory and socialist theory are based on. They are based on the collective power of the people: their irrationality, their unpredictability, the virtual impossibility of any structured technological force to stand against them.

People who animate "the public" in the same way are calling attention to an exactly opposite phenomenon. They are talking about a standardized normative insistence on how we behave in public—our socialized behavior. "Public" is how we behave when we are being civilized. This is exactly antithetically, dialectically the opposite meaning of the term "people." Individuals follow the rules of polite, civilized behavior in public. Collectivities aren't always civilized.

So we have these two notions: "public" being an animation of some sort, a word we give to human collectivity, and "public" being a place that we go out into. But I think both of these definitions are limited. I think "the public" is not a place that we go out into, but is instead the behavior that we engage in when we are in such places. This may seem like splitting hairs, but when someone says "the public," it's a contraction, like the word "it's" for "it is." It's a contraction for the phrase "the people collected and behaving in a public place." It's a contraction for "behavior in a public place." Now think of that behavior in a public place as stuck together with the little hyphens that make it all one word. So "the public" for me is "behavior-in-a-public-place." It's not identical to a public place, because "the people" behave in public too. And they do not have any characteristics of a public. They are not rational; they are irrational. They depend on raw brute power. It's not just the place itself, but it is rather what the place does to us when we are in it. The courtroom itself is just a room. It's our response to that room that creates the feeling of publicity and participation and our coming together in a collective. When I talk about "public" against Dewey and Habermas, I'm going to go against their assumption that we can collapse the concept of "people" into "public." I don't believe we can. People attempting to be powerful are rarely rational, and when they are rational they are rational on their terms, not the terms of logicians and philosophers and mathematicians.

Conversely, when we are in a public place, behaving in a public place, our rationality is a guide, a mask that we put on—insect repellent, if you will, for self-protection. It does not represent us or what we are capable of. It represents instead the system of rules which we are willing to obey in order to avoid the pains that we think might attend someone we don't trust interacting with.

The people have the power to make rules, and they don't have to be rational rules. We make some very irrational rules. Think how irrational, technically irrational, equality is. It is a stupid principle. We can take any group of people we want to and observe them six ways from Sunday, and there is no way we can define precisely how any two of those people are equal. But we insist on equality. Now who insisted on equality? "The people," who were pissed off. "The people," who were angry and intimidated and insisting on how they be treated and conceived. They are the ones who created the principle of equality. The raving mobs of the French Revolution, the mobs of people in Boston and Philadelphia who underwrote the Constitution, the mobs of people who revolted against the Stuart monarchy in England—they are the ones who insisted on equality. It is nonrational, but we have made it into a rational principle.

The power of the people is a sovereign power. It comes from within them. It is the nature of the collectivity. It's like the old Popeye cartoon. Just before Popeye gets ready to eat the spinach he says, "I've had all I can stand, and I can't stands no more," and then he eats some spinach and takes some action. That's "the people." When the people arise, they are Popeye, who "can't stands no more."

The thesis of the theory of the people is that the reality of power is always collective. Constitute government how you will, Evanberg says, infinitely the greater part of it will be left to the uprightness and prudence of ministers of state, because it is through the example, the rhetorical leadership, the moral correctness of the leaders of state, and their ability to inspire people to self-sacrifice, that the power of a state is mobilized. Any nation that attempts to go to war without the support of its people—in other words, without having collectivized itself and gotten people attuned to what is going to happen—is going to lose the war. There is no greater example of this than the recent Persian Gulf War. I don't believe that Iraq ever had a ghost of a chance against the coalition formed against it, and it certainly did not have a ghost of a chance without collectivizing itself.

There is no way that a community is going to collectivize

itself with a gun at its head. I can get people to do a lot if I just simply say, "The interests of the group require that you give up control of this part of your subject." But I am never going to get you to do that with a gun at your head. I'll get you to shut up. I'll get you to cringe in the corner. I'll get you to turn red and get the veins to stand out on your neck, and you may not resist me actively, but you won't collectivize either. No one will collectivize at the point of a gun, and no power really comes from the point of a gun. Power comes from the solidarity of the people who are asked to pull the trigger, not from the technology that they use to defend themselves or to commit aggression against others.

SUBJECTIVITY AND ONTOLOGY

There is no doubt in my mind why the intellectual problem of subjectivity has arisen today to preoccupy people so. Since 1950, we have systematically dismantled privatism and individualism in the United States. We have been breaking it down at every level — not just on the left, not just in universities. In 1950, the idea of passing a law to keep a man from beating his wife was unthinkable. Literally no one would have thought to do it. Not that anybody approved of wife beating, mind you, if it were brought to public attention in church or wherever. But no one would have thought to pass a law against it, to authorize the police to come into somebody's home to stop violence. Today we can't think of not doing that. The difference between the two is a redefinition of the dialectic of public and private.

Since we can't have a conception of publicity without a dialectically paired supposition of privacy, we can't possibly think of ways to change the public life or pass laws to change the lot of women for the better unless we can also theorize a sense of privacy. And since we can't locate it in the social institution of the family any more, because that dehumanizes a woman and puts her in a position of patronization or patriarchal subordination, the move now is to theorize the body as the locus of privacy. We are trying to find the space that we can theoretically, practically, and politically define as private. Except for the communists and the socialists, no one has ever made an issue out of privacy. The only reason privacy is an important intellectual concept is that it helps theorize the public. We can't theorize the public without theorizing the private. We theorize the private in order to fence it off and leave it alone. Once we call something "private," we say we aren't going to interfere; we aren't going to theorize; we aren't going to interpose our power; we aren't going to let people search it; no police are going to go there. The private is what we leave alone and let be—just let it go "naturally."

With theories of subjectivity, we are asking: "What is the limit of feminist theory?" "What is the limit of political responsibility?" "What is my duty with regard to political correctness?" "Where do I begin and my political and social responsibilities end?" In order to do that, we have to theorize femininity. We have to theorize a space of subjectivity for the individual. And what is that? It's nothing more than saying, "This is private. This is where politics end and where I begin." This, to me, is very important because it stands in opposition to all those people who define humanity as social animals.

Human beings are not social animals. Human beings are fundamentally individuals. We start out as individual biological organisms. That is our natural state. Whenever we form groups of any sort—bridge clubs, societies, mass movements, anything—we are assuming an artificial or acquired identity. Human society or human collectivity is the acquired behavior. The individual is the baseline behavior.

During my graduate years at the University of Iowa, philosophy was dominated by logical atomists and positivists, and the whole history of metaphysics was virtually concealed from me. We had a course in the history of philosophy, and it was very clear for that instructor that philosophy was a progression from ignorance to smartness, and smartness was atomism. So the whole notion of ontology, which is the first great branch of metaphysics, was left out—virtually repealed.

I remember when I went to work at the University of Alabama, I met a man named Max Hoecut in the philosophy department. And I was absolutely shocked. He had, in the fashion among the hippies of the time, one of those old DayGlo signs on his door that said "METAPHYSICIAN." Here was a guy who was practicing metaphysics and dared to say so. I remember being surprised by this, because although we were into ontology, nobody knew that. We were just starting to develop ontological theories.

The whole movement that we see in the field of communication and the field of literature, in all of the human sciences—say, from 1970 to 1990—has changed a lot. And it's been almost exclusively the process of continuing a self-education. People discovered from a problem that they were trying to solve that they were into an area where they had to do some real thinking about X, and then discovering, "Gee, lots of people have thought about X before. There's a whole thing here called 'ontology.'" It really has been a process of discovery for everyone.

I worry about that, in terms of part of my mission here at Iowa. Part of my mission is confessedly, unabashedly, to train the next generation of the professorate, because that's what we do here. But, you see, we are presenting to graduate students in our classes the conclusions of our meditations and researches, and we're not putting them through the same process of discovery that we went through. So I'll throw Heidegger on the desk to some surprised and soon-to-be-thoroughly-intimidated graduate student, and say, "Read this." I didn't know who Martin Heidegger was until I was practically tenured. I worry about that.

Even the social construction of reality is an ontological topic. Ontologists are concerned with the theory of being. That leaves epistemology for later. When you were a child, someone said, "What do you want to be when you grow up?" You said, "I want to be a nurse," or whatever, and you regarded the whole educational process as a process of "becoming." We talk about it constantly in that way. So the question I want to ask is this: "Is it really possible for you to 'become'? Is it possible for reality to 'become'?" If your answer is "Yes," you're a social constructionist. If your answer is "No," you're a naturalist. But it has nothing to do with epistemology. The only connection with epistemology lies in the fact that ontology is prior to epistemology.

Epistemology is traditionally foundational. Given a firm starting point, a place that we can be sure of, we can reason the following, and the following is epistemology. There has always been doubt about what that firm starting point was. Well, it was the business of ontology to settle on what that firm starting point was. Then we came to conventional arrangements. For a while we thought the starting point was God, and then we decided that the starting point was nature, and then we decided that the starting point was physics, the model science. But that is the traditional relationship: Ontology is prior to epistemology. Ontology establishes the foundation from which foundational epistemologies proceed. There's nothing really original about that. That's Descartes's move. Except I turn it around. He said, "I think, therefore I am." I say, "I am, therefore I think." It's the same move.

The real revolution in epistemology these days is conducted by the people who are arguing for theories of knowledge that require no foundation. That's what the Project on the Rhetoric of Inquiry (POROI) and the rhetorical turn are all about. They presuppose an ontology where nothing is objectively real, where everything is presented to the human mind as a construction. That's why philosophers object to POROI so much, because they think that POROI is saying that if we learn how to talk better in communities, we'll be able to get a person to Jupiter quicker. And of course that doesn't happen. It doesn't have anything to do with nature. Nature is sort of set aside.

I always assumed that the fundamental reality was the human being, and that the construction was society. It never occurred to me, until I saw people actually making the arguments, to switch that around. That's why I guess I was so much attracted to Ortega. His presentation in *Man and People* was just a presentation of what I took for granted. It is bound up in my commitment to individualism, and to privacy, because I began to understand that the thing that matters most in human communities is the comfort of people. Would to God that all Americans were couch potatoes, because those are very comfortable people. Would to God that we could have a society where everybody could afford to be a couch potato. They may not conquer any new stars or invent a cure for cancer, but they're happy, and that's what it's all about. So my commitment to individualism and my belief that the fundamental reality is the person go hand in hand.

Marxist social theory is based on the belief that the community is the fundamental reality—that the fundamental reality is that human beings are social animals, and that individuals are cells in a social organism. But where does the individual stop and the group begin?

I was really impressed with Jürgen Habermas's treatment of this question. I probably appropriate some ideas from him, which I feel I can do because he steals everybody's ideas. His suggestion is that every human being has what he calls an "ego identity" and a "group identity," and that these relationships are in a dialectical tension with one another. The fundamental reality, as far as he is concerned, is the group. The group establishes norms and rules and power relationships to discipline individuals in terms of their ego identities. And each one of us develops a sense of personhood or individuality by engaging in this dialectic with the group.

There are some difficulties with this theory, and I want to make some modifications to it. First of all, an individual is a member of so many groups that it's misleading to talk about a paradigmatic relationship between the ego identity and the group identity based on the notion of "the group." For example, you are a woman; you're a college student; you may be Catholic; you may be Republican; you may belong to the League of Women Voters and twenty-five or thirty different organizations, each of which has its own discipline. And the interesting thing that we get from Althusser is that in any particular ideological system the disciplines work together hegemonically so that one group will have its own discipline, but there will be certain preconditions that will be the same for all groups. In a liberal system, for example, it will be very difficult to find a group that will seriously restrict the freedom of speech for its members. You'll find groups like white supremacist organizations that would love to restrict freedom of speech for other groups, but it is the rare group that will abridge freedom of speech for its own members. The groups may restrict situations where free speech can be exercised; the boss won't permit the underling to disagree without losing the job sometimes. But within the underling's work space, where he or she is actually contributing to the ongoing work of the economic group, there will be freedom of speech and other freedoms too.

Sometimes you have the government stepping in to insure these hegemonic commonalities among groups by things like insisting on due process. You can't even be kicked out of your church without something resembling due process. The state will step in and make this happen. And there are probably more informal commonalities among the groups in these sorts of hegemonically similar disciplines that are culturally programmed. There probably is going to be a bias in favor of the mother tongue, whatever language you're born with. There probably is going to be a dominant gender bias. A man in a quilting circle might have as much difficulty as a woman on the board of directors of Aramco.

Those hegemonic things are there. But what really interests me about the multiplicity of groups with regard to this account of things, is the place where they are not hegemonically reinforcing one another. You may, for example, become involved with the Socialist Workers' Party, and this group is notorious for throwing out people who are not politically correct. They've been almost suicidally self-destructive ever since they were first conceived; it's a sort of Trotskyite organization. You can belong to this very leftist organization at the same time that you are a Catholic, a college professor, and a doctor's wife (and we can just load up with other very conservative organizations). But you're also a member of the Socialist Workers' Party. All the things in these other real conservative organizations that militate to dictate a particular kind of subject position for you, a different particular kind of subjectivity, are in a sense always already subverted by this weird eccentric other group that you belong to. This may be a hypothetical case, but I've talked to an awful lot of people, and almost everybody I talk to belongs to some group that is in their eyes marginal. There is no logical explanation for this.

I think it's a search for liberation; I think it's a search for emancipation. I would predict that there is one group to which you have belonged or do belong and feel fondly about that is what we used to call "cognitively dissonant" or "radically inconsistent" in some way with the other groups that make up your individuality. This membership in a marginal group is relative; it is marginal in relation to other groups. In other words, it could be just going to the bar on Friday night with the boys. And it's the presence of this in most people's lives that leads me to believe that in a liberal society, we have some way in which to insure that we can have latitudes to join the groups that we want to join. That freedom is frequently exercised, I believe, by choosing an organization that is in some way radically inconsistent with those we feel we have to belong to or are inclined to belong to. This creates slippage, so that even if it is the group that is disciplining us to give us our own sense of identity and individuality, this discipline is controlled by the individual to a degree through the multiplicity of groups—particularly the inconsistent groups—that one can belong to. It gives us some control, some slippage, over the group's disciplines—control that lets us put our own stamp of personality and individuality even on an individual identity that is coded for sociability.

The point of all this is to argue against not only Habermas, but also the more radical Marxist people who were talking about individualism being entirely an individual construct. I'm willing to go along with this, but only if they have a very sophisticated conception of ideology, which acknowledges the individual's contribution to this ideological construction and the degree of manipulation that is available to him or her.

When we talk about ego identity, I like Ortega's description with the Spanish word *ensimismamiento*. It really can't be translated, but it is usually rendered as "in and beside oneself." It's a fundamental principle of phenomenology, and it's not unique to Ortega. It's in Martin Buber; it's in almost everybody who talks about how self relates to other. Basically, the notion is that you don't really have a sense of yourself as an individual until you have contacted the other. If you can imagine a feral child, or babies at an early stage of development, they have no sense of self because they can't think of themselves as a self except in relation to others.

The phenomenological point is that I know who I am in relation to you and construct the identity that way. But Ortega modifies this, and he says, "No, what you see of yourself in relation to someone else isn't your real self; it's a construction. It's a construction of the you in relation to the other, so that you are describing yourself as you think you might be seen in the other's eyes. And that is really a you; it's an identity, it's important. It's a persona, but it stands beside yourself."

The reason this is so attractive to me is that it is responsive to the people who suggest that the individual is a totally illogical construction. This position that I get from Ortega stands against the ideological people, because if we say that the very recognition of self at that radical level is ideological, then the concept of ideology loses all meaning. We are talking about a phenomenon that is so close to pure cognition, so close to the reasoning capacity itself—the ability to see position A in comparison to position B and trying to estimate what the other is thinking—that ideology loses all meaning. There's no contact with the state at all in that kind of a conception. The concepts of Freud and different levels of consciousness are so radically basic that ideology just loses its meaning.

For me, what Ortega is establishing is that Habermas and the others have it wrong. There is a relationship between ego identity and group identity, but it's not the group identity that's primary; it's the ego identity that is primary. You can tell the story either way. We can say that you are constructed by your society and you engage in political activity in order to emancipate yourself, and you are free to the degree that you can find your own ego identity, your own subjectivity. Or we can say that you have an ego identity or a subjectivity that is disciplined very harshly by the groups to which you belong, and that you achieve your emancipation by choosing to withdraw from groups whose discipline is uncomfortable to you, and by choosing other groups that subvert the structure of groups to which you belong. And you achieve your emancipation by preserving that which was yours all along. That is distinctly Ortega, right in the beginning of *Man and People*.

Two of my favorite scholars are Helene Cixous and Julia Kristeva, and at one time they were fast friends, but they disagreed radically on this particular question. Cixous went one way and Kristeva went the other way, and now Kristeva is in the position that Simone de Beauvoir was twenty years ago. She's *persona non grata* among the people who once were her biggest fans and allies. Kristeva and de Beauvoir made about the same move that I made in saying that there's an ego here, at some radical level. This is a position that is associated less with Continental phenomenology than it is with American pragmatism. What we have is a story that is told that is much more like G. H. Mead's *Mind, Self, and Society* than it is like either Freud or Lacan.

But it's not the same. I don't think that American pragmatism's attitude toward society or individuality can really be captured without having gone through what we've gone through with Continental theory. We can't go back to G. H. Mead and John Dewey, because they didn't have it right. They had some things right, if we put it in the right political and economic context. A real good handle on this is the notion that Mead had, this wonderful totalization that he believed was a thoroughly transparent society. And nowadays those of us who are holding positions close to Mead hardly ever use the term "society." We talk about "groups," plural. Our understanding of society is based on the heterogeneity of groups, not their totalizing homogeneity, and that makes a big difference in the symbolic interaction theory.

Chapter Six

Materialism

"Materialism" is a coherent philosophical position that is a variant of realism. Philosophical realism generally treats ideas as being real in themselves. If I can think the idea of freedom, for example, I'm going to treat it as real. And the degree to which I can't recognize it or find this idea, or realize it through my activity, is the degree to which I'll dismiss it as a dream, or a fantasy, or a myth, or a lie, or something that's not real.

Historical materialism consists of coded human practice. Its semiotic tracks are representations, and these tracks become sedimented over time in "binding observances," as Ortega y Gasset would call them—meanings that we agree to agree to, that we agree to live by, to observe, and that we regard as binding upon ourselves and upon others. And this binding quality of them makes them abiding and permanent in a way that ordinarily we don't think of language as being. Ever since the medieval empiricists started inventing shortcuts for the rule of causation and challenging nominalism, we've come to have the notion that words are merely the counters for things. And we separate things and meanings from the terms themselves without understanding that they're really all bound up in one another and that they're *always already* determined.

Materialism is tied to the nature of language, and calls at-

tention to the distance between ideas and the words used to express them. We think of liberty as the *meaning* of the word "liberty,"
rather than as an idea that's independent of the word and the
meaning. A thoroughgoing philosophical materialism looks at
all ideas in their material manifestations and does not assume
that they have any existence above and beyond their material
manifestations in language and as discourse. As a coherent
philosophy from the moment of its founding, materialism was
the epitome of secular humanism. It refused divine intervention.
It refused divine definitions of ethics and morality and held human beings responsible for themselves—for conducting themselves in a humane, ethical, and moral way.

Karl Marx's criticisms of the prevailing democracies in the
beginning of the industrial revolution of the last century were
not arguments for communism, but were social analyses of the
British Empire in the period 1840 to 1850. Every criticism Marx
made pointed to a moral deficiency of the state, whether that
had to do with child labor laws, safety standards in working situations, or substandard pay. All of the things he was calling attention to he believed would agitate the proletariat to throw off
their feudal and capitalist masters. And they were all things that
came to him out of a humane and moral impulse. But in the
United States, because of the vision we have of communism since
the "Red scare," we fear a dictatorship of the proletariat. We make
equivalent the regimes of Stalinist Russia and fascist Germany,
Hitler's Germany. There are a lot of remarkable parallels. Both
governments tried to run by terror; both governments tried to
impose solutions in ways that did not work out. But the impulse
that lies behind Marxism is quite different from the impulse that
lies behind fascism.

Behind fascism is a desire to glorify the survivor in a sort
of grand survival-of-the-fittest warfare. On the other hand, the
impulse behind Marxism and socialism has been to eliminate
"man's inhumanity to man." If you read Soviet literature—even
during the height of Stalinism, where it's nothing more than a
shallow rhetorical excuse to send marginalized people to the
gulag—you still find Soviet leaders obliged by their own rhetor-

ic and their own people to develop their arguments in terms of the phrase "man's inhumanity to man."

We can consider the most extreme kind of materialism on the right—what I guess we'd want to call a vulgar materialism of the capitalists, in which one steels oneself in an Ayn Rand way to achieve whatever is necessary to make one happy, and that which is ethical and noble is simply that which encourages one's growth as an individual. This is a fascist notion that runs counter to the moral impulse that's part and parcel of materialism. It's a Nietzschean vision. It's a vision of humanity as being able to get beyond good and evil. And I don't think this is possible. Humanity is never going to get past good and evil, because humanity as a collective consideration, and as a collective entity, consists in and of its goodness and its evil. Other than that, we're simply just a bunch of individual organisms.

Then there is classical Marxist materialism that talks about two different worlds—a world of ideas, and a world of matter—and takes a position with regard to the precedence of one over the other. Marx, for example, will say that it's possible for one to think from the heavens down when he's criticizing Feuerbach's book. The classic political Marxist is aiming toward an understanding of the world in theories, ideas, philosophies, plans; these are mental activities, clearly separate from either language or the reality of the world itself. But I believe that we must think from the ground up, from what we can know that real, thinking, living human beings do. And then we ascend to the heavens from there. The starting point should be real and material, rather than scriptural, textual, or ideal. Whatever ideas are developed should be reifications of or abstractions from what we experience empirically in our world.

I don't believe that there is such a thing as an idea independent of language and discourse. I don't believe that language and discourse are mediations. I believe that language and discourse are the things themselves. Basically, I am denying that language mediates. I am suggesting that there is no mediation; there's merely a physical, objective, out-there world, and then there's language and discourse. Everything that we think of as ideas and mental

activity is nothing more than playing around within the structures that are already provided for us by language and discourse.

Clearly, a short story is "created" by an author who puts it
on paper. But the story is real; it's material. It can be told and
retold. It can be performed orally. It can become mythic. It can
win a Pulitzer Prize. A l kinds of things can happen that are necessary consequences of the story. We're not talking about two different realities, one material and the other one symbolic or mental.
We're talking about two different kinds of material realities. We're
talking about a material reality that's physical, and the study of
it will help us get a rocket to Jupiter one day. And we're talking about another materiality that is discursive rather than physical, and it won't help us get a rocket to Jupiter, but it will explain how we construct and structure our own minds and societies
and cultures. It is historically material rather than physically
material.

We can talk about the materiality of language by looking at
a piece of paper that has notes on it and ask what the materiality is of these little purple scratches on this white paper. They
are the matter. They are paper and ink, and I've moved the ink
n a certain way, and I could say that there's meaning in those
scribbles. But the physical part of it is really apart from the meaning. This is a demonstration that a lot of philosophers, rhetoricians, and theorists of language used for a long time in order
to show that meaning and ideas were things that hid behind
words — that language concealed. In fact, however, I don't believe
that I invented any of those words on that paper. Those words
all existed before me as what the Saussurean linguists call *la langue*.
Each of them has a history of usage.

Further, I'm in communication, if only with myself. I'm in
communication, because those notes are going to do me no damn
good whatsoever if I can't make out what the chicken scratches
say, and if I can't use the chicken scratches to reconstruct what
it was that I wanted to remember. So I am contributing to my
own empirical history, my own biography. I'm contributing to
the meaning of why it is that *philos* means "philosophy," or "w/"
means "with" when I'm taking shorthand. All these meanings are

conventionalized. Our unique combination of words in our own sentences is simply a restructuring.

The soul of creativity is deconstruction and reconstruction, but it's not inventing things. It's reforming things, restructuring things, finding a new angle on things. But not in terms of invention. Because all of the possibilities of meaning are already encoded in the history of the language, its usage; in the history of the culture, its contextualizing; and in the history of society, its constraints. What makes it this way, of course, is history, long usage, the binding observance. What makes it a usage is the fact that it's been done over and over again. If we simply invent a word, "nowklumpschnugel" or "glittersnatch," and give it a meaning, and we get a whole bunch of people to agree with us, it will become a binding observance and a usage, as measured simply by the number of people and the amount of time that the term signifies what it claims to signify.

Every figure of speech, every term in the language, every story that's ever been told, and every argument that's ever been made dies in the same way that a dead metaphor dies. We still use it, but from a sociocultural viewpoint, it's far more significant that rhetoric's arguments and figures are dead, because when they're dead they're constraining. When our friends in the English department say that a figure or metaphor is dead, they are saying that it is trite and they don't like it. Or they are saying, "Well, that's a technical term, but we can come to appreciate its creativity by recovering the sense in which it was once a live metaphor, even though it now appears dead." They are valuing the liveliness of metaphors.

It's almost like we've got our metaphor for metaphors backwards, because a metaphor really becomes alive when it becomes what we call "dead." A truly dead metaphor is a creative metaphor that someone might use in an English class as an example of how creative writing ought to be done. That to me is not alive, but dead, because it has no audience; it hasn't communicated anything. It doesn't say anything. It's still a creature of the author's mind and the reader's fascination. It has no conventional meaning. No sheer determination. Historical materialism is purely linguistic. It is conventional; it is a determinate. It's a binding observance. Even though it is a linguistic form — something as small as an ideograph, or as large as the Gettysburg Address — it has acquired such an abiding permanence that it's more like a rock than a poem.

OBJECTIVITY

Human discourse is neither referential nor subjective, but both at the same time. Objectivity remains important; objectivity has clear meaning for us. But it means, "Bracket the moral, set it aside; bracket the religious, set it aside; bracket the historical and the traditional and the political and the ideological, set them aside. And now let's see what we can do with the problem." This can have important results. Almost all of medical science is a product of this sort of procedure.

But when we fetishize this procedure — when we say that everything that we have bracketed must never again be returned to, and bracketing means throwing out and not just simply bracketing — we are throwing out every human dimension of truth. And this is one of the tremendous catastrophes of humankind. Secular humanists have been so schooled this way that we don't even like to use the word "morality," let alone study it and insist upon it. Why is that? Because we have let a useful invention — objectivity — become a stereopticon, a tyrannical machine, that constitutes what it should only enable.

I think our problem is an interesting theoretical problem. We know what scholarly writing looks like. We know what its earmarks are. The key feature is the footnote. And here we're after precision — precise knowledge in the sense that the person is an expert and really knows what he or she is talking about, and can send us to his or her sources. But by contrast, in scholarly talk there aren't any footnotes. So the question is, "What is it that makes a scholarly conversation different from political punditry? Or a conversation over coffee between well-read truck drivers? And, again, what are the markers of scholarly talk?" In writing, we are concerned with having knowledge in a different way. When I'm writing, my books are right at my hand. I have notes, and I have notecards. In other words, I don't necessarily *command* the knowledge that I have. I can go and find it, or I have it at hand in some way. But in a scholarly conversation, whatever knowledge is put into the conversation must be commanded. It has to be in my head, memorized in some way—at least in some form or another.

Precision isn't as important without the footnotes. For example, I think that the month of March in the system that was introduced in France after the revolution is *Brumaire.* I know that Louis Napoleon gave a speech attacking the French Institute that Marx made much of in writing his own critique and essay on, but I can never remember the exact date. I can always talk about it, but I could never publish in writing any of the talk that I have about the something of *Brumaire,* because I don't "know enough." And yet when I talk about it, no one objects to my talking about it with imprecision. I can make sense of it, having read it and understanding a little bit about where it fits. In scholarly talk, there's almost a requisite imprecision, as it were—the expectation that we're interested in the *meaning* of the knowledge more than the knowledge itself. The conversation that we're involved in is actually putting the knowledge to work.

Most people don't have all of their *t*'s crossed and *i*'s dotted when they call up a bit of evidence from their memory. They'll have the wrong day; they'll have the wrong year; they may even have the political parties switched in the stories they are telling. But it doesn't make any difference. Because they finally wind up with a proper interpretation. They've made an interpretation of basically a flawed text, as it were—a text that we could show is wrong in some way. But if we corrected the text so that it was right in all of the particulars, the same interpretation would be made of it. So when people forget particulars, they are not forgetting what matters, because it's the interpretation, it's the meaning of the knowledge, that matters. A lot of intellectuals claim expertise on their ability to cross *t*'s and dot *i*'s, rather than on their ability to show what their knowledge means. But its importance is how it relates to the world and how the world ought to use it.

Most people develop an overall interpretation, an impression, a judgment of what it is that they learn before it is ever, shall we say by metaphor, "textual"—before they understand all the *t*'s and the *i*'s. They then check their work, check back over their impression. That's when they start crossing the *t*'s, dotting the *i*'s, and learning the specifics. Five years later, they won't remember to check back with an accounting procedure. They'll remember the interpretation, and the interpretation is always right even if the facts are wrong.

If I have a fact, and I have it in writing here in front of me, and I look down and read it, I'm never going to be wrong, in terms of facts. But with regard to the way people actually interact rhetorically, what they remember is not facts, but what the facts mean—what they interpreted the facts to mean; how important they were; what they did with them; how they related the facts in some way to action or belief. And *that* they remember correctly.

INSTANTIATION

Materialists are always caught in a terrible association with either communists or Wall Street. To say that people are materialists is to say that they value money—that they can't talk about such things as love and honesty and integrity and ethics and all of the higher and finer things in life. Well, this is, of course, bullshit. It's not that a materialist doesn't think about or talk about these ideals or these abstractions; it's just that a materialist insists that you talk only about abstractions that can be instantiated, rather than talking about abstractions that are empty or hollow, that cannot be instantiated. To say that it *can* be is to say that it *is*. A rhetorician would be more intent upon using the word "are" than the words "can be." In philosophy and philosophical disputation, it would count only that you imagine a case where that would be true. In rhetoric, you have to point to a real case where that's true.

An example of this is the notion of class in the United States. Class is not historically material in the United States. I don't mean that there are no classes; there are. But we have been ideologically deluded into believing in the absence of classes to the point where we don't know how to behave as a class. The groups to which people belong are not such totalizing abstractions. You belong to the Rotary Club. You join the American Association of University Women. You work as a banker. These are the groups that you are conscious of belonging to and that, considered together, equal society. When I say that I am a member of the Knights of Columbus and I am a member of the middle class, those statements are not commensurable in signaling group membership. The first statement does signal group membership, with very real implications for action, consciousness, and behavior. The second statement is simply an acknowledgment of place or position within a hierarchical structure that we have been taught describes our society. It doesn't have any real behavioral implications. If anything, the perception that one is classed becomes a primary motivator for seeking out these other groups. Someone says you're middle-class; this is a great way to get you to go to a labor organization meeting. Someone says you're an elitist; it's a great way to get you to wear blue jeans. Someone tells you you're low-class; it's a great way to get you to put on a tie.

Class is, in a sense, a huge abstraction. Most Marxist theorists, particularly Western Marxist theorists, are backing away from it a lot. I don't want to say that there are no rich people. I don't want to say that rich people do not act in their own interests. I do not want to say that rich people acting in their own interests do not screw everybody, because they do. The point is that this is not a class conflict—even though class itself has some historical materiality, because Marx invented the term and used it rhetorically, and Marxists have used it rhetorically ever since.

But from a rhetorical viewpoint, these class differences don't make a difference in any demonstrable sense. You can explain all of Marxist theory, including historical materialism and class conflict and the struggle for the superiority of the proletariat, without ever mentioning the word "class." You can say "workers," you can say "factory owners," and that's where the fight really takes place from a rhetorical viewpoint. The term "class" is an abstraction.

"Instantiate" is an important word for anyone who is a materialist, because a materialist has to deal with a whole realm of "ideas" that idealists have been talking about for years, because they say these words can't be discussed materially. They suggest that we can't be empirical about liberty. A philosopher can talk ideally and draw all of these schemes about what "liberty" is, but I can tell the story of liberty and point to a particular activity that particular people engaged in at a particular time, and say, "*there* is liberty working." And unless I can do that, it doesn't exist for me. There's no "angel" for me. I've never seen an instantiation of "angel," so anyone who is seriously inquiring how many angels can dance on the head of a pin is deranged, because there's no possible instantiation in my world view of this abstraction.

The word "instantiate" comes from "instance." In Spanish, the word "instance" is *instancia*. They don't say "instantiation," they say "*instanción*." It's much clearer when it's connected with the word "instance" in Spanish than it is in English. Too many people use the term "instance" as a synonym, for example. But an instantiation is a particular that embodies and illustrates an abstraction. So, for example, if a philosopher is talking with a materialist or a realist about something that is as abstract as the soul, the philosopher will be asked, "What do you mean, 'soul'? There are a lot of useless things in the human body, like the appendix, but what part of the body is the soul?" And the philosopher is required to respond and in some way give an example.

We must tell a story about a particular practice or activity that someone has engaged in. Though we may not be able to point to a particular part of the body that is the soul, we can say that this activity that people engage in establishes that they have souls. An instantiation is any concrete manifestation of an abstraction. Abstraction is a huge general category. It would be accurate to say that "chair" is an instantiation of the abstraction "furniture."

If we draw the line between theory and practice, we would tend to confuse the terms "instance" and "example." An example is an argumentative term. An advocate or an arguer will make a generalization. All generalizations, as we know, are both untrue of any particular in the category, but at the same time (and apparently contradictorily) true of all members of the category. If I say that the average depth of the lake is 4.7 feet, there may be nowhere on that lake that measures exactly 4.7 feet. What I have said is untrue of any point of the lake, but at the same time it is generally true of the whole thing. The word "example" would refer to the part–whole relationship between a generalization and the number of particulars collected within it.

Frequently, a generalization is expressed as an abstraction. The term "furniture" does indeed *generalize* the objects we call by that name, but the logical operation isn't the same. Giving an example is reasoning by induction. Seeking an instantiation is having arrived at a conclusion by deduction or inference in some way, and seeking to understand whether it exists in the practical world. Technically, an instance would be my ability to point to a real-life activity or practice of some sort that I thought exhibited a quality that I had arrived at through inferential or deductive *a priori* reasoning. An example, on the other hand, would be one of the particulars that in a scientific mode I had consulted before I arrived at a generalization that covered the range of the things I was studying.

An example is any instantiation of an abstraction. Abstractions are not examples, unless they are more particular than other abstractions, in which case they can become examples. A sentence that is typical of some poststructuralist might be something Lacanian like this: "Woman is inscribed in such a way that for her, *différence* is the only possible thing, for there is no positive condition." This is a very confusing phrase. And right at this point a rhetorician might say, "I understand your words. I think I understand what you mean. Can you give me an example?" And what would be wanted in this case is an example of some creature that fit the signifying range of the term "woman," who had no positive existence of her own, but was instead defined by negation or by *différence* in relation to other known identities. An acceptable example would be anyone who was called Mrs. Husband's

Name. In this case the abstraction is a complex phrase that represents a generalization, even an argument in a claim, but it makes it far more clear to me when I am given the example. So, for instance, we refer to "Mrs. John Smith" rather than "Jane Smith."

If I then confine the entire philosophical argument to the case of someone who uses her husband's name instead of her own, I'm being reductive. But the purpose of logic is to be reductive. The purpose of argument is to be reductive. It's to produce understanding. The question is not whether I am being reductive, but whether I am being reductive in the proper direction. If I do encapsulate this entire philosophy in the example of Mrs. Husband's Name, will I make any mistakes? Well, of course I will. And as I make my mistakes in working this coordination between the argument and the example, you are undoubtedly going to point them out to me. And as you point out my mistakes, you will point to another example to capture my mistakes. And another and another. By the time we work through our dialogue, I will have an understanding. I will never exhaust all of the possible examples, because I will only push you for additional examples until I reach the point where I understand you.

One of the ways to keep academic or intellectual conversations from becoming mental masturbation—intellectuals talking to one another, more about counters than about things—is to insist upon a criterion of clarity. And a criterion of clarity does not mean that you only count as knowledge or you only acknowledge what a farmer in Tennessee or a steelworker in Gary would recognize. We're not after clarity in that sense. But we're after clarity in the sense that Kenneth Burke calls "realism" and I call "materialism." The sense that if you're going to talk about a problem of identification, it should be the problem of identification that X human being, for whom the sign "woman" is a designated attribution, faces in Y culture at Z moment in history.

The problem of the theory of the subject can never be settled in principle, and this is the main issue that separates me, and I think most rhetoricians, from French discourse theory. In France there is an attempt to settle the problem of subjectivity in principle, as a kind of generalization that will apply to all instances of human subjectivity. In rhetoric there is an attempt to confront the problem of subjectivity in specifics with regard to how people see themselves — what they are willing to do and to be at a particular moment — as opposed to what it would be *better* for them to do and to be in order to achieve their goals in life. The problem of subjectivity is very specific, and when the rhetorician always insists that you say "for example," this has nothing to do with objecting to the form of the argument.

We underestimate the compass. The compass is one of humankind's greatest inventions. It always points to the north, and we know that if we have to find our way around the desert or the oceans or any place else, we need a compass. And in order to find our way around the world of ideas, we have to have a compass too — something that lets us not just be where we are, but understand where we are in relationship to other places we might be.

"For example" forces people to introduce into their scholarship a different kind of discourse that is more accessible to people without specialist training. "For example" does not take the place of the technical language of the difficult argument, but it provides another place for us to be — a moment of coordination, where we can work out the difficult theoretical language in terms of the example, or the example in terms of the difficult language, in order to negotiate where we are.

This leads us to consider the difference between English and communication — between literary studies or a belletristic tradition and a rhetorical tradition. And the difference is over the value one places on communication. Is communication itself a value, or is expression a value and communication an accident? Rhetoricians tend to regard expression as an accident — "Oh, I could have said that in any one of fifteen ways" — and communication as the goal. In English and in literature, it's the expression that is the goal, and the substance and the communication that are accidents: "I could only say this in one way. This is the only way this could be articulated."

Communicability is producing discourse that crosses, that

bridges human beings, that integrates human lives. Being expressive, in my view, is almost narcissistic—finding self through the manufacture of discourse, pleasing self through the manufacture of discourse. And so people who are taught writing as self-expression rather than as communication, whatever else they gain by it, are culturally and socially handicapped by the very process of their learning that way.

In a similar vein, a materialist believes that knowledge is as knowledge does. It operates in and on the world, not just in university classrooms. An example of this is Alfred Nobel, who invented dynamite. He did it very precisely in his laboratory. He understood all the procedures that he used. He could tell us the precise mixtures that were necessary. He studied it six ways from Sunday and gave us a thorough scientific description of all the facts that were relevant to the creation of dynamite. This was over 100 years ago. Dynamite is currently being manufactured in a number of places, and some of the people making it dropped out of high school. They may not know what a molecule is; they don't know the history of what they're making. But they're making a higher-quality dynamite than Alfred Nobel did.

Both a sophisticated chemist and these people have knowledge. Both of them can make dynamite. A sophisticated chemist can know how to make dynamite, and a high school dropout can know how to make dynamite too. They know it in different ways. The question is, which one takes precedence? Suppose I have a room full of workers here who are coming to me complaining about their health, saying that they have been making dynamite for fifteen years and they've all developed pancreatic cancer. And I say, "Well, bullshit. None of the chemists have shown me that there's any connection whatsoever between pancreatic cancer and the manufacture of dynamite. Let's listen to the experts." That response is saying that these people are not experts, which has always seemed really silly to me, because they are experts. They make dynamite for a living. If that's not an expert, what is?

We see this all the time. Chemistry is not what the professors say it is. Chemistry is what we do in light of the knowledge we call "chemistry"—what we do because of or due to what we know about chemistry. There are people with all these various compartments of knowledge, and these compartments of knowledge are not filed away in a dusty library someplace, simply existing for the convenience of scholars. They are used to doing things in and on the world. And, importantly, it is not usually the academics who do things with the knowledge.

A MATERIALIST'S MORALITY

Although a materialist insists upon examples of knowledge acting in the world, that does not eliminate all forms of idealist thinking. We must have ideals; we must have values; we must have dreams. The key to a materialist ethic or a materialist fantasy world is that these dreams have to be practical. They have to be, in a sense, realistic dreams—dreams that could come true. It would be very idealistic of me to envision a world where all human beings agreed to the point where there would never be conflict. But I think it is a practical, achievable goal to find a world where people agree that any resort they make to violence is a confession of their own incompetence—where they believe that when conflict does arise, their inability to negotiate it, to talk it out, to end it without resort to violence, is their fault, their incompetence, their failure. There still will be times when violence is necessary. But we'll be violent with a heavy heart and with a downcast eye. And when we win this conflict, as we recently won the Persian Gulf conflict, we don't wave flags at home. It's totally inappropriate. We wear black for the thousands of people who died over our collective incompetence. That to me is a realistic dream—something that I can project in the future with enough of the markers of something that could realistically and practically come to be.

Utopian thinking is not a legitimate subject for the materialist, because utopia urges you to think without the fetters of practicality. It urges you to think about an ideal state—not one that we can achieve, not one that's realistically possible, not one that would ring true, but one that simply represents a negation or an inversion of our current perception of social and human problems. Every dream about the future needs to be a realistic fantasy, one that is pragmatically possible in some time frame. It doesn't have to be in our lifetime. We should be thinking in generations, not decades, when it comes to social change. There must be a reasonable expectation that achieving this dream is a possibility. We can see the road to it. And we can tell people where the road signs are. We know where its curves are and where it is straight.

I don't want to put any fetters on human imagination or human dreaming. I only ask that when we start building collectivities and changing and moving social orders and bending and fracturing culture, we keep in mind that we must have some object in doing this, some goal. And the goal cannot simply represent our desires, but our desires *and* our resources, our capacities, our ability to adapt to unforeseen turns in the road. We can't cling to a utopian model with a single-minded vision and an uncompromising attitude.

Utopian thinking is typically uncompromising and measures everything against its ideal. And the little compromises that we have to make in order to realize some or most of what we want in life always fall short of this utopian vision. For the most part, a compromise does not destroy the object of our striving; it has merely made it more attainable. And we must embrace the compromise, work with it, go with it, and see where it will get us.

Unlike Kenneth Burke, I don't believe that the human being is "rotten with perfection." The human being is blessed and stimulated by an *urge* to perfection. It's not rotten. It has an urge to perfection. The problem, of course, is that we take this urge to perfection and try to make ourselves into demigods or gods instead of human beings. So we imagine what a demigod or a god would be able to achieve with regard to a state or a condition, and we hold ourselves responsible to that standard. We can't do that. We have to talk about *human* perfection. Human perfection, if you're a batter in baseball, means that two-thirds of the time you fail to do what you're paid to do. Because if you hit .333 you're going to be the National League batting champion. That means one hit out of every three times at bat, or two failures out of every three times at bat.

A materialist ethic also must be based upon the attainable. I don't envision any human ever being Jesus. I'm not sure Jesus was Jesus. But I do hold human beings responsible for what I think human beings can achieve. I don't think that's unreasonable. Knowing the difference between right and wrong doesn't even require a smart person. All it requires is seeing a large person strike a small person, or seeing someone yell at someone else in a tyrannical fashion. Virtually every human being knows at the moment of that occurrence that it's wrong.

In practice, I believe most human beings, and in fact most dogs that I've known, have a highly developed moral sense. Two dogs are fighting, and one of them starts to get hurt; first thing it does is turn belly up and whimper. When a dog does that, no other dog will kill it, with the possible exception of a pit bull that's been bred that way. When a human being whimpers, cries, or gives signs of pain and discomfort, every other human being, I believe, in a practical situation, has a natural nurturing urge to find out what's wrong and what can be done. If you see someone being hurt or hurting, you understand that this is a condition that should not be. If you witness it, you even can feel the strokes and the pain somewhat yourself. You have a natural impetus to intervene. Regardless of the nature or justification of the violence, the moral impulse is to stop the violence, stop the hurting, stop the pain. And I don't believe that we have any difficulty recognizing other human beings in pain. I don't believe we have any difficulty whatsoever understanding that we have an impulse to stop the pain. We do not have any difficulty with the practice of morality.

But with the invention of writing, we decided not only that we had to have a philosophy about morality, but we had to write a book called a philosophy book. And in order for it to be serious philosophy, we had to go through certain procedures of argumentation and footnoting and interpretation and soul searching in order to put all of this in writing. It's the putting it in writing that's hard, because it abstracts morality from practice. How do you put in writing your feeling when you see somebody being hurt and your urge to stop the pain? How do you put that in writing? I can tell you a story, and that's about as close as I can come. I cannot argue this propositionally and justify it as a rational act. As a matter of fact, it is frequently a very irrational act, because I put myself at all sorts of risks by intervening to stop people from hurting—whether I'm protesting capital punishment or trying to stop a rape. All kinds of harm can befall me as a result of acting on moral convictions.

The Christian morality through history has proven, if nothing else, that it is thoroughly idealistic, thoroughly utopian. It represents what only some people can reasonably hope to achieve. Take, for example, the Pauline epistles in the New Testament that urge us to go forth and multiply, but we must do so within the bonds of holy matrimony, only where approved. This whole line of argument is giving people one avenue, one way to go, that only a very few can follow. Others will want to sow a few wild oats. Others will want more than one partner in a lifetime. Others will want a sexual partner without children. Others will want children without a permanent sexual partner. Human approaches to the problems of family and procreation are variable in every direction, by inclination.

If we create a society where every style of dealing with family and procreation is prohibited except one, Christians believe they will have created a true utopia. And, of course, Christianity is very up front about this. Christianity has created a world of sinners It defines a category of sinners by creating a situation of not sinning that is virtually impossible for anyone to live, and creating institutional signals that that's exactly what they're doing. There's the confessional booth in the Catholic Church, and if you don't go to the confessional booth to confess a sin, then clearly you're lying. You're keeping something from your priest. The world is structured in such a way that you create sinners. I don't believe in sin. I think that this whole Christian notion of sin is psychologically and socially very unhealthy for humanity.

I tend to focus too much on the question of human desire when I think about the notion of right and wrong, and I should think more about different obscene conditions. Maybe I'm too much of a pigeonholer. But I think of some questions as primarily political, and some questions as primarily moral, and some questions as primarily rhetorical or representational, and so on, depending on how I want to treat them. And to me a problem such as the homeless, while clearly obscene, is more political than it is moral.

The distinction between the political and the moral is in regard to one's personal activities or subject positions. If you intend yourself, personally, to act, then you're taking on the moral role for the people. You're taking on the responsibility of making a power claim. These are people who are involved in picketing. These are people who are driving nails for Habitat for Humanity and directly addressing the homeless situation. That's moral. They are taking action.

Politics is when you're going to think about it—when you are going to engage in a lot of discourse consumption and production, and you're going to organize and choose leaders, and you're going to delegate someone else to deal with the problem. You think of the problem as more remote. You don't think of it as having any direct connection to you, certainly not requiring your activity or leaving the comfort of your own house or your own couch. You are instead willing to live in a republic and let the representatives in a representative government represent you, as long as you have your say and remain a part of the public. The public is the realm or the space where politics operates to measure each one of those claims against the individual who is making it and what he or she is doing with himself or herself.

The notion of morality for most of this century came to revolve exclusively or primarily around one's personal sexual behavior and anything that could be compared analogically or metaphorically with it. I know it was the case when I was growing up that if you walked up to a woman and pointed a finger at her and said, "You are immoral," and seventy-five people witnessed this communicative interaction, it would be absolutely clear in seventy-five people's minds that someone had just accused her of sleeping around. If you walked up to a man and pointed your finger and said, "You are immoral," the same seventy-five people would believe that he was cheating on a woman in some way. It is a positive step when we get rid of that primary association and work the analogies backwards. Instead of saying that what is obscene about pornography is also obscene about the homeless, we should ask, "What feeling do you get when you see the homeless?" And then, "Can you see this in pornography or a film or a movie or a book?"

I believe that the two people most successful in dealing with this are Helene Cixous and Julia Kristeva when they discuss the whole notion of abjection as the origin of the obscene. If you say that the moral impulse in humanity is to resist abjection, it's a very material grounding for an ethic, and in a sense it shows you what the abyss is in the real meaning of the word "abyss." What is the abyss? It's the rotting corpse — the sure sign not only of your own mortality, but of the disgusting pus and corruption that you become when you are no longer inhabiting this world. It's this vision of abjection that defines the human moral impulse as the resistance to abjection. Every time you see a buzzard floating in the air, yell at it and say, "Not now, you son of a bitch." That is resisting abjection.

If you take that kind of an attitude, then it becomes really a political thing. It helps you not only in dealing with fantasies and desires and evaluating your own realistic and unrealistic fantasies; it helps you also in making moral judgments about political things by establishing a pretty good standard of what it is that you find objectionable about any social condition. And this is the ground for persuasion. It is not a ground for jail terms and fines. Our society has become entirely too dependent upon jail terms and fines and legalistic proceedings and suing this and suing that. The difficulty is that we've forgotten to be rhetorical. We've forgotten how to put claims on one another that don't have jail or a fine or a point of a bayonet as their bottom line.

Part Three

A PREVIOUSLY UNPUBLISHED WORK

Chapter Seven

Fragments of Winter: Racial Discontents in America, 1992

I recently promised to amplify the claim that critics and theorists should emphasize the term "rhetoric" more than the term "criticism" (McGee, 1990). This essay honors that commitment. I suggest that performative criticism sensibly responds to the postmodern condition. My original strategy was to theorize performative criticism, using brief examples to show how useful the approach could be. Published responses to my first essay, however, convinced me that a detailed illustration of what I have in mind should precede rather than follow a theory of performative criticism. More "cloud hopping" at this stage would not dispel the notion that poststructural thinking transformed me into "a hermeneutic Indiana Jones who makes it up as he goes along" (Gaonkar, 1990, 307). I judge that only a performance of performative criticism can respond sensibly to those who are wary of using rhetorical methods in scholarly work. I am confident that a clear case of the work critical rhetoric intends will correct the impression that I propose making "the rhetorical scholar indistinguishable from the street rhetorician" (Condit, 1990, 339–42, 345, note 29). To demonstrate my academic intentions, therefore, and to illustrate performative criticism, I will "finish the text" of the Rev. Dr. Martin Luther King Jr.'s oration "I Have a Dream."

After finishing my first essay (McGee, 1990), for instance, and while working on this project, I was invited to a special program of the 1990 Southern Speech Communication Association (SSCA) convention in Birmingham, Alabama. David Zarefsky, Michael Osborn, and I spoke from the pulpit of the 16th Avenue Baptist Church, where three children were killed in a bomb attack in the 1960s. Zarefsky was assigned to speak about Abraham Lincoln; Osborn was asked to talk about King; and I was asked to judge the influence of King's dream on American liberalism. Although our audience was composed mostly of academics, and we were sponsored by an academic organization, there were enough devices of true publicity to make each of us feel that we were in a moment of danger. We spoke from the same pulpit King had used. Martyrs had died there. African-American parishioners were present. A television camera recorded the event. Although all three of us are practiced performers, we all experienced unusual performance anxiety. We were in no real danger, of course. No stonemason sat in the corner to engrave our words as we spoke. No police officer stood in the back waiting for one of us to utter a damning phrase. But we felt something momentous in the occasion, and we spoke accordingly. When three rhetoricians who take their work seriously huddle together in that situation to speak of Lincoln, King, and American racism, how can they help but feel the foot of the elephant?

In terms of the present project, my Birmingham assignment was to deliver a public speech on the relations of an "unfinished text" and a constellation of fragments representing changed racial beliefs, attitudes, and actions (McGee, 1990). My discourse had to be both a performance and a criticism. It had to make a scholarly point (a "serious" point, one representing knowledge), but it also had to be itself rhetorical — an oration and not "an essay standing on its hind legs" (in words attributed to James A. Winans; see Caplan, 1962). My own understanding profited from directing this discourse to an actual rhetorical situation. This should not be understood as necessary for performative criticism, however. Performative criticism can be written in cloisters, even published in dusty journals. The difference between reflection from the subject position of philosophy and reflection from the subject position of rhetoric lies in an orator's anticipation of performance where elephants walk. Anticipation of danger, more than the anticlimax of actual performance, makes oratory one of the more fearsome, anxiety-producing human activities. Write as though you were speaking, and speak as though you are under the scrutiny of a tyrant. You will then be in harm's way, where elephants walk.

Critical rhetoric is useful for hermeneutics because of its capacity (1) to reflect; (2) in anticipation of action; (3) while actually, or "playfully," in the presence of power. The more invisible a vigilant power is, the more critical rhetoric helps. No one can see or understand all of the elephant from trunk to tail. You see only the foot, the imminent threat, the fragment of the beast that poses a moment of danger for you. Understanding power is thus always a question of interpreting fragments of it. If the three of us made sense in Birmingham, it was because of our skill in interpreting fragments while in a moment of danger. I claim that we have this skill because we are rhetoricians: Rhetoric has always been a study of influential fragments mobilized as a response to exigent situations (see Bitzer, 1968).

Since ancient Greece, rhetoricians have been able successfully to divide their art into two general categories of skill and substance. The skills of rhetoric are what one must practice to achieve excellence of expression. The substance of rhetoric is what one must study in order to produce discourse that will have influence in the world. Rhetoricians deal with substance under the headings of invention and judgment. Their study consists of collecting and grooming fragments to be cataloged for future use in rhetorical performances. They learn the maxims, the proverbs, and the commonplaces of their culture. They learn the currently fashionable ways of talking about history, economics, politics, ethics, law, social relations, and discourse. They are sensitive to their environment, collecting examples, remembering them before they are even sure about what the examples are examples of. In the past, this meant keeping a systematic record of commonplaces. Today, it more frequently involves broad training in the liberal arts and social sciences, as well as the universal activity of "doing research" at the library. Doing research in argumentation is the intellectual equivalent of making gravel at a quarry. It consists of making little rocks out of big rocks, of reducing large pieces of discourse to important fragments. We say that fragments written down on 4 × 6 evidence cards are "the main points" of the larger discourse, "the argument in a nutshell," or "the bottom line."

"FINISHING THE TEXT" OF "I HAVE A DREAM"

For good reasons or ill, it is not uncommon for fragments to become far more important than the whole discourse from which they emerge. Just as the concrete highway made from gravel is ultimately stronger than the block of stone from which the gravel was made, so fragments recombined into other discourses may be stronger than they were in their first context. Political consciousness is, in large part, a new structuration of "quotable quotations" from the leaders of the republic. We learn as children that liberty is more important than life; that there is nothing to fear but fear itself; and that black is beautiful. We also have gatekeepers who certify the significance of discursive fragments. Recently, for instance, E. D. Hirsch Jr. (1987) was distressed that American children appear to know the wrong things. To help them get it right, he and two friends quarried the history of Western civilization, alphabetizing the gravel in *A Dictionary of Cultural Literacy* (Hirsch, Kett, and Trefil, 1988). Workman Publishing Company in its turn has crushed this impressive proof of the postmodern condition into 365 numerically ordered fragments, a "shoelace 1991 calendar" titled *365 Things Every Kid Should Know!* Here, on the disposable, recyclable, tearaway page for January 15, we learn that King's whole oration is less significant than its most frequently repeated sentence: "I have a dream." We even learn which particular repetition of this sentence culturally literate children between the ages of seven and eleven should remember. It is a fragment within a fragment: "I have a dream that one day this nation will rise up and live out the true meaning of its creed: 'We hold these truths to be self-evident: that all men are created equal.' " Not only the whole speech, but also King's life, and the material forces the shoelace calendar calls "the civil rights movement in the South in the 1960s," lie in the meaning of one compound–complex sentence.

We remember King—or Martin, as I shall refer to him from now on—in a messianic persona. His life as a peacemaker is, like the life of the Prince of Peace, a text that inspires oppressed peoples the world over. He proved that an empire without a dream lacks the cultural solidarity to withstand principled resistance from within. Early Christian martyrs mobilized religious solidarity against the sovereignty of the Roman Empire and ultimately took control of Rome itself. I would like to tell a simple, parallel story of Martin's dream, providing the moral solidarity needed to confront and to capture racist Washington. It would be good to think that legislation passed in 1964 and 1965 will eventually end racism. But I cannot dwell on a long-dead field of honor. Interpreting presence with an eye only to the past sells the future short. Moreover, in this instance, it also results in a lie. My grandmother taught me never to tell lies, especially in a church hallowed by the blood of martyrs, or on the printed page.

Martin's dream was a culmination of the romantic civil rights movement. In many ways, the 1963 March on Washington was as much a watershed for American cultural life as the student uprising of May 1968 was a watershed for French cultural life. Both make interesting responses to those who need the comfort of an arbitrary historical marker "ending" modern politics and "beginning" postmodern politics.

In modern politics, the most important feature of society was its structure—the pattern and meaning of its institutions, its governing part, and its laws. The secret of political success was organization, an ability to get out the vote that translated easily into the power to write laws and the right to enforce them. Enlightenment consciousness understands everything social within organic metaphors. Democratic theory was "natural," foreordained either by a deity or by some deistic personification such as "history." In this figuring, social problems are perversions "nature" never intended. Thus, founders of the republic "had their hearts in the right place." The contradiction of professing equality while owning slaves is "not their fault." It is even superficial and relatively unimportant in the sense that it is reparable through tinkering with underlying structural causes that "determined" Thomas Jefferson's immoral behavior. Notice how such thinking assumes that victims must pay a price for their relief, while the sociopaths who bully them are tolerated. To claim that the problem lies deeper than the surface is to suggest that marginalized citizens, even slaves, must tolerate their victimization in anticipation of achieving human birthrights as delayed gratification.

Consider the "disease" metaphor, for instance. If racism and bigotry are "diseases," we must search for a way to eliminate these and other social practices that can be figured as "viruses" or "germs." And in the meantime, we overlook racism and bigotry! We make apologies for racists and bigots by assuming that their actions are beyond their control in the same way "catching a cold" is beyond human control. We then seek "medicine" capable of working a "cure." Since all "medicine" takes time to work, victims of racism and bigotry are urged to be patient, even to the point of tolerating continuous abuse from those who have not yet been affected by the nostrum. We can argue against this figure from within it by suggesting that since "medicine" has not worked in the past, we have no reason to believe new "medicines" will work in the future. Structural changes meant to "cure" racism and bigotry, it seems, have the effect of perpetuating, even sophisticating, the "disease."

By contrast, the postmodern condition forces a "superficial" perspective on social problems, presenting them as questions of representation. We should not think in terms of the "disease" metaphor or any other structural formula, because such figures are themselves the source of error. Bigotry lives on the surface of society, in the appearance made by discourses used to privilege one group over others. In practice, people resolve the question of identity ("Who are you, really?") by associating with some groups and dissociating themselves from others. This is done through a series of signs. Sometimes the signs are linguistic and the association purely discursive, as when someone says, "I am an African-American," or "You are not a Native American." At other times, the signs consist of appearances made by what seem to be personal choices. Living in that neighborhood, for instance; working here and not there; going to this church; and doing that for fun are all representations of identity. Bigotry is the habitual practice of identification-by-negation. Whenever you claim that you are what you are not, you say little about your Self except what can be inferred from your attitude toward people you do not like. If this becomes your sole, primary, or dominant means of identifying yourself, you probably are a bigot. In this way of thinking, you are as responsible for your bigotry as you are for what you say. Dealing with bigotry is as simple — and as difficult — as insisting upon changes in the way people signify human groups and so represent themselves.

So far, limited experience of the postmodern condition seems to suggest that political success will lie in mastery of the hyperreal world of political communication. The term "hyperreal" refers to images that are "more real than real." Within an Enlightenment consciousness, discourse was said to be a "mirror of nature." "Being realistic" about political problems thus meant worrying about creating discourse adequate to "reflect" political realities, perhaps to "capture" them with camera-like accuracy. Today, if you are a politician, "being realistic" often entails changing your identity, behavior, and opinions so that you embody some larger-than-life discursive representation of yourself, your "image." Constructed images are hyperreal in that they are more heroic (or diabolical), more exciting (or pedestrian), and more courageous (or cowardly) than your actual character, as measured by conduct, could ever be.

George Bush's conduct, for instance, suggests that he is a cautious, careful man. In the "image wars" of contemporary politics, this trait becomes "the wimp factor." Bush is frequently said to be motivated by a desire to resist the term "wimp." To "talk tough," he cultivated an association with a larger-than-life film character, Dirty Harry, repeatedly telling opponents to "read my lips" as he promised "no new taxes." When circumstances forced him to break that promise, his "spin doctors" urged the public to interpret this contradiction between word and deed as "political courage," more evidence that George Bush is not a wimp. In late 1990, several interpreters speculated that the failure of diplomacy to achieve the liberation of Kuwait might be attributed, in part, to Saddam Hussein's conviction that Bush is in fact a wimp who would not risk war. After the Persian Gulf War, some analysts claimed that the greatest benefit of the war for Bush was the demise of his wimp image. If we focus on how the Enlightenment version of democratic theory functions, we hope that a "realistic" political question would ask, for instance, "Is it wise to continue deregulating banks in the wake of the savings and loan scandal?" Today, in an emerging "postmodern" version of democratic theory, truly "realistic" political questions pose hyperreal problems: "Will I appear to be a wimp if I back down now on my promise to deregulate banks?"

Representational politics are manifested everywhere, not just in theorizing social problems or translating "images" into "issues." Major legislation now comes in multiple volumes, written in such language that it can only be understood as it is represented in slogans and in simplistic media "analysis" of its "main points." Furthermore, liberal visions of the "loyal opposition" have turned to pablum. Confrontation between "ins" and "outs" rarely occurs, and when it does, public attention often centers on a symbol of opposition. So, for instance, Democratic senators who appeared to oppose Republican Supreme Court appointment strategies were in fact satisfied to torpedo the nomination of Robert Bork, and then to surrender the right and obligation to oppose. Either our problems are so new, or our perceptions of them are so different, that we seem to have no way of dealing with them except to "just say no" or to "declare war." Saying no and making war are alike in their fundamental abandonment of the notion that structural adjustments can resolve social problems. The culture of the melting pot is fractured and fragmented. We operate on the clear supposition of cultural diversity, where one's identity may lie more in ethnic or racial determinants than in Lincoln's dream of a house undivided. The question to consider in understanding the fate of Martin's dream is thus different from what is necessary to understand the dream itself. The dream itself, a creature of modern politics, was a vision of the consequences of dramatic structural change. The fate of the dream, on the other hand, is being determined by the value it has in representational politics—the political economy of the sign.

REPRESENTATIONAL POLITICS AND THE PROBLEM OF IDENTIFICATION

If I had to list all of the discourse fragments that give Martin's dream currency in postmodern politics, I would be writing for a very long time. Happily, I think I can do the job by featuring Spike Lee's brilliant film *Do the Right Thing*. The film is a discussion of Martin's dream, and the less visionary rhetoric of Malcolm X, as influential fragments in a practical, localized political dispute. The film is brilliant not only for its sensible discussion of the present texture of racism, but also for its crystallization of the technical term "representational politics." It practices representational politics in the act of portraying representational politics.

Do the Right Thing calls attention to its own nature right away, reminding us that life is awash with titillating cultural fragments competing for our attention, our allegiance, and our money. A woman we will later know as Jade, our hero's lover, is decked out in boxer's attire and dancing to a Public Enemy performance of "Fight the Power." Jade never stops moving, striking out in every direction at an invisible opponent, never making contact. She enacts a representation of her Self determined by her vision of a sport. All sporting events provide model identities. Spike Lee's hero, Mookie, suggests knowledge of and respect for historical African-American role models when he sports Jackie Robinson's baseball jersey. Another prominent character wears "Magic" Johnson's Los Angeles Lakers jersey. A white yuppie who has bought a cheap house in the neighborhood, in hopes of "reclaiming" it, wears the Boston Celtics jersey of "great white hope" Larry Bird. Other fragments, from television, flash through my mind to "confirm" Lee's association of sports images with potentially racist identities. I remember a salt-and-pepper television commercial where Bird and Johnson, in their basketball costumes, "compete" to sell shoes. In another commercial, Bird and Michael Cooper of the Lakers "compete" to sell beef. I also remember the sportscaster fired for characterizing Bird's limited jumping ability as "white man's disease," and another announcer who was called to task for describing Detroit Pistons star Isiah Thomas's practiced professional skill as "natural athletic ability."

In the world of athletics, at least, there is an attractive representation of one thing it could mean to be an African-American. Not so in the world of fast food. The beaming face of Colonel Sanders is white. To find an equally well-known black image, we have to go back to the 1930s for the much less flattering association of Aunt Jemima with pancake mixes and syrups. The stores in Spike Lee's Brooklyn are white-owned fast-food restaurants and Asian-owned fast-shop groceries. The major set of *Do the Right Thing* is Sal's Famous Pizzeria, a neighborhood institution where virtually everyone comes daily for a slice or two at $1.50 each, $2.50 for extra cheese. Sal is very Italian. He built his business twenty-five years ago, when the neighborhood was predominantly white. Now he lives in Bensonhurst and drives to work every day in a white Cadillac. (For an account of the significance of locale in *Do the Right Thing*, see Sullivan, 1990.)

Sal's Famous is a family business that employs Sal's two sons as well as our hero, Mookie. Sal's sons are reflections of the two sides of their father's nature, representing the two faces of white liberalism. The younger son, Vito, enjoys his work, his friendship with Mookie, and the community's grudging acceptance of him as a part of neighborhood life. He and Mookie are friends in the colorblind vision of Martin's dream. Vito is the son of the Sal who courageously stayed in a decaying neighborhood with the oppressed minority who make Brooklyn their home. The elder son, Pino, on the other hand, is a bigot who hates his job and worries about what his Bensonhurst friends think about his working in the ghetto. He seems at first to compete with Mookie for his younger brother's affections. In time, however, it comes clear that he wants only to dominate Vito, much as he seeks to dominate black "Brothers" in the neighborhood. Pino is the son of the Sal who drives home in a Cadillac after paying Mookie $250 for six ten-hour days. Sal's tolerance for Pino suggests that bigotry can hide in one's character, inside what we are willing to accept as representations and enactments of any mode of Self (in this case, Sal's projection of himself into the future through his "flesh and blood").

The difficulty with Sal's white liberalism, therefore, is neither the contradiction between where he lives and where he works, nor even the contradiction between what he says and what he really thinks. Mookie is willing to live within the economic and political rules of the dominant culture. He is an unwed father dependent on his sister's ability to pay the rent, and he has no visible prospect beyond working for Sal. He is nonetheless committed to hard work, even for meager pay, as opposed to the alternative of sitting on the corner with "Sweet Dick" Willie to watch the world pass by. Mookie is not ignorant of his interests. He understands Sal's negative side (Pino), and he thinks he can subvert it by cultivating Sal's positive side (Vito). The main conflict in the film thus arises in the structure of racial representations, not in the inequities of America's economic and political infrastructure.

A POSTMODERN ARGUMENT
FOR FAIR REPRESENTATION

In tension against the faces of Sal is an African-American trinity fixed in the first character we meet. Smiley opens the film with a direct address, breaking the plane that ordinarily separates film from spectator. He is mildly retarded and handicapped by a

speech impediment. He is the picture of innocence, the very opposite of "streetwise." Smiley accepts without question the romantic story of heroic black knights in shining armor solving the
problem of racism in the 1960s. In halting, stuttering speech, he
transforms his heroes into commodities. He attempts to sell us
a black-and-white snapshot representing Martin and Malcolm as
joyous, smiling comrades-in-arms. Viewers know immediately that
Smiley dwells within his own romantically distorted vision of
history.

We meet the two faces of Smiley's snapshot one at a time,
as they become embroiled in the film's conflict. An excitable
young man with the improbable name of "Buggin' Out" is a
representation of Malcolm. He comes to Sal's Famous with not
quite enough cash for extra cheese. He tries to negotiate with
Sal, but he fails as Sal reminds him of his fixed prices—prices
as inflexible as all other structured rules of the Enlightenment
world. Buggin' Out is frustrated, spoiling for a fight; knowing
he cannot win by Sal's rules, he moves his quarrel to another plane
where he has a better chance. Rather than complain about the
price of cheese, he chooses to argue about representations. One
wall of Sal's Famous is decorated with the same type of black-
and-white photographs Smiley has tried to sell us. Sal calls it the
"Wall of Fame." The photographs are representations of Italian-
Americans whose images capitalize Italian ethnicity. Perhaps
prompted by Smiley's recent attempt to sell him a representation of Martin and Malcolm, Buggin' Out confronts Sal with the
fact that "you ain't got no Brothers up on the wall here." Sal
responds defensively, with the same argument he has used in
refusing to negotiate the price of extra cheese. Invoking his right
of ownership, he says: "You want Brothers on the Wall of Fame,
you open up your own business, then you can do what you wan-
na do. My pizzeria, Italian Americans up on the wall." Buggin'
Out calls attention to the consumer's stake in any economy: "Sal,
that might be fine, you own this, but rarely do I see any Italian
Americans eating in here. All I've ever seen is Black folks. So since
we spend so much money here, we do have some say" (Lee with
Jones, 1989, pp. 141–42). Sal threatens Buggin' Out with a base-

ball bat, and then banishes him on the grounds that he is a
troublemaker.

Offended, hurt, Buggin' Out responds with a strategy appropriate to modern politics. He says he's going to organize the
neighborhood to boycott Sal's Famous until African-American
pictures are hung on the Wall of Fame. People in the neighborhood will not cooperate, however. They are accustomed to representational racism, especially among white liberals. They have
taught themselves to overlook it, and so condone it. A white liberal, after all, is preferable to a redneck bigot, even if he is insensitive to representational racism. Yes, it's patronizing, but Sal pays
the elder sage of the neighborhood beer money to sweep the front
sidewalk. True, his interest in Mookie's sister may be as lascivi-
ous as a slave owner's nightly visits to the slave quarters. But it
could also be interpreted as care for neighborhood youngsters
who have grown up eating his food. Yes, Sal's eldest one chased
Smiley away from the store in a barrage of racist epithets; but
did not Sal intervene, publicly punishing his son?

However, Smiley, hurt by the incident with Sal's eldest, is
ready to listen to boycott rhetoric. Buggin' Out also finds an audience in Radio Raheem, a representation of Martin, the third
face of the African-American trinity. Raheem is physically im-
posing. He fearlessly walks the streets carrying the loudest, fan-
ciest, most expensive "boom box" in the neighborhood. He has
found his representation in music that enables him to "Fight the
Power" simply by playing Public Enemy loud enough for all to
hear. In addition to his radio, Raheem sports two fashionable
four-fingered brass knuckle rings. The ring on one hand spells
out "LOVE," and the ring on the other spells out "HATE." Raheem
makes sense of the world by using his rings, and his knowledge
of boxing, to figure life's struggles. "HATE," he tells Mookie, goes
on the left hand because it jabs at you, jabs, jabs, jabs, until you
forget about the right hand. In the end, however, "LOVE" sees an
opening, and delivers the decisive blow.

Raheem identifies so closely with his musical representation
that he has let it become his name. He carries it with him proudly, testing his radio's power against that of rivals as if he were

involved in a manhood ritual. He comes to Sal's Famous to order two slices, his radio at full blast. Sal tells him to turn it off or leave. Once again, Sal asserts the structural right of ownership by arrogantly informing Raheem that there will never be music in Sal's place. *"Capisce?"* Sal asks, forcing Raheem to acknowledge his humiliation nonverbally with a nod of the head. Raheem's only gesture of resistance is to wait until Sal has put the slices in the oven before ordering extra cheese. But he is ready to boycott.

A CLASH OF STRUCTURAL AND REPRESENTATIONAL POLITICS

Through the course of the film, Mookie comes to represent everyone in the neighborhood who does not want to get involved. He is caught between two character clusters: the competing white liberal and African-American trinities. He seems tolerant of the surface of each trinity, apparently confident of his ability to manage Sal's and Smiley's claims on him. He avoids contact with the more violent, aggressive faces of each trinity, attempting to maintain a civilized but distant relationship with Pino and with Buggin' Out. He nurtures the intimate relationship he has developed with Vito, and he is fascinated by Radio Raheem. He believes that the African-American trinity is right, but he has no reason to take representational politics seriously. After all, neither photographs, words, nor music will feed his child or break his bones. He understands that the rhetorical power of his general life strategy—playing the two faces of white liberalism against each other—nearly always works to his advantage.

The final confrontation of the film occurs at closing time. Sal has had a long day, a record hot day, but a good day for business. Despite all his confrontations, he is feeling good, ready to forgive all those who have transgressed against him and his property rights. When Sal feels better, all the world is supposed to feel better. He shares his dream of the future with his sons and with Mookie. Much to Pino's chagrin, he announces his intention to rename the business Sal and Sons' Famous Pizzeria. He promises that Mookie will always "have a place," for he has "been like a son." Mookie thus gets another perspective on representational politics. The young African-American, the very simulation of a son, has worked hard to learn a trade. Perhaps he has a dream of one day owning his own business in his own neighborhood. Then he hears Sal account for him, magnanimously, as a perpetually patronized hired hand. Mookie shrugs it off and concentrates on drawing his pay.

After Sal locks the door, four young revelers arrive to beg for an after-hours slice. In his mood of self-satisfaction and contentment, Sal lets them in over the objections of his sons and Mookie. On their heels come Buggin' Out, demanding African-American faces on the Wall of Fame; Smiley, with his photographs of Martin and Malcolm; and Raheem, with his radio at full blast. In the face of yet another confrontation, Sal's mood shifts. When the boycott trinity does not leave, Sal produces a baseball bat and proceeds to pulverize Raheem's radio. Not only is Raheem denied his representation in Sal's Famous; he is also forced to witness the destruction of his only way to reproduce musical representations (and thus to "Fight the Power"). Raheem responds violently to his symbolic death. "HATE" grabs Sal and yanks him out from behind the counter. "LOVE" and "HATE" get a tight grip on Sal's throat. Everyone is rolling on the floor. Somehow the tumbling tangle of humanity rolls into the street in front of Sal's Famous. The neighborhood gathers. Someone calls the police.

The police have been represented in the film as reluctant enforcers of white liberal rules. They have been inclined to ignore the letter of the law in such minor violations as opening a fire hydrant to provide neighborhood children with some relief on the hottest day of the year. They do not want to get involved in the ordinary street brawls to be expected when tempers flare. If an official complaint is filed, however, they will enforce the letter of the law. The police wade into the fight in front of Sal's Famous. They succeed in pulling the participants apart, and they handcuff Buggin' Out and Smiley. But Radio Raheem offers too much resistance. One officer succeeds in prying Raheem's hands away from Sal's neck, but he loses control of himself in the heat of battle. Fellow officers try to restrain him, but he will not release the billy club he has across Raheem's throat. Necessary force becomes deadly force as the enraged officer chokes the life out of Radio Raheem, killing a representation of Martin as viciously as James Earl Ray killed the man himself. Fearing more violence, the police pack up the corpse and their prisoners and rush away, leaving a crowd stunned into silence and inaction.

Mookie, who has been neutral in the conflict all day long, now comes to a new understanding of representational politics. Representations are rhetorical; they persuade people to be and to act in ways they might not otherwise contemplate. Representations have important material consequences to the degree that they successfully influence people. A simple request for representation (no pizza without representation!) has resulted in the system-sanctioned murder of a young man. When confronted by representational politics, white liberals have resorted to deadly force. Calmly, deliberately, Mookie picks up a trash can from across the street, walks over to the display window of Sal's Famous, and does the right thing. He smashes the window and leads an angry crowd in the important business of trashing and then burning Sal's Famous Pizzeria.

Curiously, given our view of what constitutes high office, the politics that matter most are worked out in the day-to-day interactions of a neighborhood. Racism in America no longer exercises the iron control of legally closed social, political, and economic systems. Today it is literally unthinkable that there be separate drinking fountains, restrooms, sports entertainment industries, and so forth, one set for whites and one for blacks. In that sense, and to that extent, Martin's dream has been successful. The breakdown of the structural features of America's apartheid, however, does not end racism. That is the lesson of the postmodern condition. Whether the problem is nuclear disarmament, pollution of the environment, the drug culture, the legion of homeless, the curse of AIDS, the tyranny of patriarchy, or the demons of racism, a structural solution is insufficient to solve it. The difficulty is that passing laws, rewriting the Constitution, or even extreme measures such as socializing the economy will not scratch the surface. The relationship between surface and depth has exactly reversed itself. In Martin's time, we used to say that representations were only surface, superficial, mere talk, mere rhetoric. In the postmodern condition, the evidence is multiplying to suggest that our world is surface. Culture, society, even our very identities are matters of representation. The surest evidence that human problems are overdetermined is that eliminating structural causes no longer guarantees the elimination of undesirable effects. To change the representation of things, that is the trick. Martin's dream now means finding a way to persuade Sal that he should buy Smiley's photograph of his own volition. He should frame it, and display it proudly on the Wall of Fame as a signal that he, his business, and his customers must live together or hang separately. He must show that he himself dwells within the most fundamental inscription of American liberty: "All men are created equal."

Why? When liberalism views representation as a governmental, structural problem, it fails to recognize that the phrase "rights of representation" has changed in meaning. Voting for representatives, of course, and apportioning legislatures, are still important events. The representatives who matter most today, however, may not be in Congress or in the White House. Images and depictions of who we think we are, and who we want to be, are totems in the world of hyperreal simulations. If we do not pay attention to totems people value, we will end up in a dither of "inexplicable" situations. Sal will kill Radio Raheem over the absence of a picture, or Raheem will kill Sal over the silence of a tape player. Either this marks the limits of Martin's dream, and also the limits of liberalism, or it marks the true materialization of Martin's dream, and of a new "postmodern" liberalism. Liberalism has rarely attempted to deny citizens what they want. The only thing it insists upon is rational process. Sal's resort to violence rather than negotiation, creating a situation where the only moral response is more violence, portrays a deaf liberalism content to let its principles become "due process" rules in courts of law. Mookie's reluctant revolutionary act holds us to a higher standard—in my mind, a more authentic liberalism. Martin marched to Washington to put his claim on a government. Mookie stays home to put his claim on friends and neighbors. Martin wanted laws to guarantee equality. Mookie wants representations signifying that equality dwells within—it is a lived practice. Martin wanted punishments and crimes rearranged. Mookie wants society-wide displays of lived equality.

In the midst of the burned-out hulk that Sal's Famous has become, Smiley carefully, reverently thumbtacks a photograph of Martin and Malcolm on what is left of the Wall of Fame. We have known for centuries that we cannot deny any people their fundamental right of representation. When we do, they rise up against us, and in the charred remains of whatever it was we were trying to protect, they will tack their representations on our wall. In the words of Brother Love, the neighborhood disk jockey who has witnessed the destruction of Sal's Famous, "That's the truth, Ruth."

JUDGMENT: THE "PARTIALITY" OF CRITICAL RHETORIC

"Ruth's truth" is of course partial, but this characterization does not mean what it once meant. Being "partial" in the past was a bad thing, and the cure was to "be more objective" by "telling the other side of the story." But what is "the other side" of Mookie's moral choice? A tale that portrays Sal as a victim? An interpretation that valorizes Sal is as easy as dropping the term "fair-minded" into the caption of a photograph: "Aiello received an Oscar nomination for his portrayal of Sal—the fair-minded, volatile pizza-shop owner in *Do the Right Thing*" (Flatow, 1990, 13). Such an interpretation freezes property rights and rights of representation in perpetual conflict. The goal of interpretation is to solve problems through understanding, not to stultify them in an understanding that never adapts. To be "partial" is thus to take sides in a moral controversy, refusing to apologize for what you find morally repugnant. I speak in praise of Mookie because he "does the right thing," and I thus reject any interpretation that would praise Sal. My judgment amounts to a claim that the possibility Sal represents is no longer "the other side" of Mookie's moral choice. I have only judged Mookie's action as an alternative to Sal's insensitivity, however. My interpretation is "partial" in the sense of incomplete until I consider Mookie's action as a praxis worthy of imitation. Judgment requires, ideally, both a relatively fixed standard (theory) and a comparison (practice). Martin's dream has become a representation of historical struggle that functions as a fixed standard, at least in the mainstream African-American community. The search for a practical comparison soon leads to the judgment that Lee himself is "the other side" of Mookie.

The African-American community has always been more aware of the importance of representations than most other minorities. On January 16, 1991, for instance, ABC televised the National Association for the Advancement of Colored People's (NAACP's) 23rd Annual "Image Awards." Actors Whoopi Goldberg and Morgan Freeman, and singer Dionne Warwick, were among the personalities receiving awards. Martin's dream superintended the event in a remarkably vivid representation of how the past influences the present, and thus of how the present will in its turn influence the future. After the pattern of the American Academy of Motion Picture Arts and Sciences' presentation of the Oscar awards, the distribution of small statues to honorees was sandwiched in between proscenium stage performances by singers and dancers. Rear-screen projection was used to display a black-and-white film of Martin delivering the "I Have a Dream" oration. This dated technology contrasted vividly with the full-color glitter and presence of a live stage show. Musicians produced a high-tech sound with a slick, driving beat that would not have been possible in Martin's time. Five young children known as The Boys, whose parents were children in 1963, bobbed rhythmically in a constant-motion dance in front of Martin's image, singing or lip-synching their recent upbeat, optimistic hit. At the beginning and ending of their performance, and between the verses, Martin was made to utter his repetitions of "I have a dream . . . " sentences to the beat of a contemporary music he never heard. Martin was a ghost, a black-and-white spirit reciting sacred words—not out of context, but in a new context.

The NAACP's honorees had at least three things in common. They stood in the shadow of Martin. Their pictures were being placed on a Wall of Fame. And all of them earn their living in the American culture industry. Spike Lee hasn't yet been included in this company, but I am certain he eventually will be put on both the NAACP's and the American Academy's Wall of Fame. His recognition will be momentous, because he is importantly different from other celebrities who have achieved star status as performers. However wealthy and visible they may become, performers remain commodities in the culture industry. Some (actors Bill Cosby and Eddie Murphy, for instance, and composer Quincy Jones) have established production companies in an effort to gain more influence over their art. Only a few have moved successfully into the business of the culture industry, however, and most of them continue to depend on their high visibility as performers. You see no African-American representation among owners of football and baseball clubs, and only one National Basketball Association franchise is owned by African-Americans. Although a majority of professional athletes are African-American, coaches, general managers, and referees are usually white. Nearly all music, television, and film production and distribution companies are owned and operated by whites. Spike Lee is therefore unique, for he seems on the verge of projecting himself into the company of Orson Welles, George Lucas, and Steven Spielberg. He is, and he always has been, a writer, producer, director, and actor all at once—an auteur who has the power to control his own creativity.

At first glance, there is an admirable consistency between Lee's on- and off-screen struggles. His films, like Martin's sermons, analyze and interpret American political consciousness. He "makes a speech" attacking some facet of racism with his every film. In life, Lee's ambitions transcend his ethnicity. He wants to be admired as a representative of the African-American community, but he wants even more to tack his motion pictures on the mostly white wall of the American Academy of Motion Picture Arts and Sciences. *Do the Right Thing* was good enough to be considered for that honor, but Oscar snubbed him. He seems, therefore, to be embroiled in another battle against representational racism as heroic as Mookie's. Putting his pictures on Oscar's Wall of Fame would signal his acceptance by a community of artists unaccustomed to thinking of an African-American as a genius behind the camera. That acceptance would constitute the destruction of another important racial barrier—an accomplishment the spirit of Martin would celebrate. To achieve this goal, he has only to make more films (presumably about some facet of racism), and to make them better. This involves, in the main, an ever-increasing flow of capital. And there is the rub: What Lee does to capitalize more ambitious films can corrupt his identification with Mookie.

Don't get me wrong. I am not about to rehearse the tired critique of "commercialism" that says Lee was less corrupt when he had to wonder where the next can of film was coming from. What Mookie does to fight representational racism is fixed within the narrative boundaries of *Do the Right Thing* and the historical precedent of Martin's dream. What Spike Lee does to fight representational racism is yet to be constructed from a number of fragments, which include everything he says or makes to accumulate capital for subsequent projects. To keep his on-screen and off-screen images compatible, Lee must live up to the moral claim Mookie so rightly lays against Sal. He must dwell within his own representations, as Martin lived the nonviolent message of his sermons. If he treats his own political representations as powerless, without social or cultural consequence, his indignant story of Mookie's moral choice could be fairly interpreted as ungenuine, manipulative, and exploitative.

Lee uses all the gimmicks other film producers have invented to maximize income in an economy that rests more on popcorn sales than on revenue from tickets. The motion picture is now only the center of a complex of related fragments offered for sale in multiple markets. In addition to theatrical release in America and abroad, the film will be offered for sale and rental on videotape, and ultimately it will be sold for broadcast on cable and free television. A popular film will also generate royalties from toys and articles of clothing that are ostensibly meant to advertise the film. If the film is based on a novel, the book will be reissued to take advantage of the publicity generated by the film, usually with a royalty-generating cover photograph from the film. If the film has an original screenplay (as all of Lee's do), a "novelization" or a book on the making of the film will appear to add to the coffers. Clips from the film, and even short documentary films on its making, will be distributed to an increasing number of television shows devoted exclusively or primarily to "covering" the culture industry in pseudojournalistic fashion.

Unlike such other *Wunderkinden* as Welles and Spielberg, Lee foregrounds himself in the industry that springs from his films. He always plays one of the main characters in his films, and the paraphernalia offered as mementos of his films are copies of his costuming. Usually with the assistance of Lisa Jones, Lee writes the books based on his productions, and they are clearly focused on the omnipresent activity of Spike Lee (see Lee, 1987; Lee with Jones, 1988, 1989, 1990). In addition to sending the more visible of his cast members on talk show circuits, Lee appears himself. He uses the opportunity not only to sell his film, but also to complain of his treatment by the Academy, to discuss racism in the culture industry, and to reply to critics who might have been kinder. He has also invented a new way to capitalize on his films: He produces television commercials, treating them as he treats feature films, insinuating himself into them in a persona he originally created for a character in one of his films.

Lee's foray into commercial television gave him an opportunity to work with one of his heroes, basketball player Michael Jordan. Jordan was America's most popular athlete in 1990 Q ratings. He is the latest in a long line of professional athletes who earn more from endorsements of commercial products than from performance contracts. His face is on the Wheaties box, and he is a prominent player in the "great shoe war," in which manufacturers of athletic footwear hire professional athletes to wear their shoes and hawk them in television advertisements. Ideally, endorsements would appear as commercial breaks in broadcasts of athletic events featuring the star himself. Viewers of a Chicago Bulls basketball game on Sportsvision cable network during the 1991 season, for instance, saw Jordan make a spectacular play that forced the 1990 world champion Detroit Pistons to take time out. During the break, Jordan addressed viewers directly in a commercial attributing his prowess to the shoes he wears. The social consequences of this sales pitch become clear when we realize that basketball is dominated by African-American athletes. These athletes are role models for young people who want to improve their economic and social condition. Young African-Americans living at or near the poverty line grow up wearing tennis shoes and basketball shoes, not because they are tickets to wealth and fame, but rather because they can be the cheapest and most durable footwear available. If the shoes are invested with representational value, however — if they come to be signs of athletic prowess and economic success — they can be among the costliest items of clothing. How much does Michael Jordan's fetish cost? What is the value of magic shoes?

Nike brand shoes have led the market for a number of years. As we might expect, Nike made the highest bid for Jordan, and in a stroke of marketing genius, the company hired Lee to film the commercials. Lee wrote and directed a series of eight Nike commercials between 1987 and March 1990. Others were appearing as of March 1991. Lee appears in each as Mars Blackmon, a character from his "1986 breakthrough film, *She's Gotta Have It*." Mars became a cult image of the African-American youth culture because of his "jazzy patter and a hilarious, hard-edged way with words" (Seymour, 1990, 29). Lee casts Mars as the quintessential African-American basketball fan. He thinks that Jordan is the best ever to play the game (a claim with racist overtones, since Jordan's competition is Larry Bird, the white star of the Boston Celtics). The motif of the commercials is Mars's attempt to find out how it is that Jordan can appear to defy gravity with his jumping ability. He watches Jordan, takes "action photos of my main man" displaying his "high-flyin', death-defyin' ways," and even consults a physics professor (Seymour, 1990, 30–31). "Is it the shoes? Is it the shoes? Is it the shoes?" Mars asks three times in his characteristic patter. And of course it is.

Lee presented himself as the solution to advertising agency Wieden & Kennedy's major problem of 1990. They wanted to feature a commercial made especially for the college basketball national championship tournament. The National Collegiate Athletic Association (NCAA), however, forbids advertisements featuring athletes who are paid for playing the sport being televised. Lee was so successful in identifying Mars with Jordan, and through Jordan with Nike shoes, that Jordan could endorse Nike shoes in absentia. In the commercial aired during the NCAA tournament, Mars shows photographs of someone's feet, implied to be but never claimed as Jordan's, "slammin' in Detroit" and "slammin' in Philly." He even shows what he calls a "[Larry] Bird's eye view" of Jordan "slammin' in Boston" (Seymour, 1990, 31). Though the spirit of NCAA regulations was violated, the letter of the rules was observed. Lee in the process transformed Mars Blackmon into a representation of Jordan: When you see Mars, you see Michael. The 1991 "March Madness" commercial has "Aladdin's genie," Little Richard, granting Mars a single wish. The wish is to "become" Michael Jordan. Little Richard says the magic words, and the camera cuts to Michael Jordan wearing a Mars Blackmon costume. When you see Michael, you see Mars. And whichever way the signifying goes, you know that the Mars/Michael identity wears Nikes. This identification makes Lee-as-Mar a valuable commodity and adds considerably to the revenue *She's Gotta Have It* continues to generate. Lee also thoroughly implicates himself in the practice of selling expensive shoes to impoverished teenagers.

Lee argues in *Do the Right Thing* that representational politics are consequential. In the filming of Nike commercials, however, representational politics are evidently neutral—just an "everybody does it" sales pitch, justified by what Lee does with the money. In this case, however, poor minority striplings so highly value the fetish Jordan and Lee have created for them that they are ready literally to kill for a pair of Nike Air Jordans. This contradiction between Mookie's image and Lee's image is not simply a critic's theoretical inference. It is recognized as an important issue of contemporary representational politics in the television series *Gabriel's Fire*, an ABC vehicle for James Earl Jones, he of the incomparable voice.

Jones plays Gabriel Bird, an African-American ex-cop who is on parole after serving twenty years in prison. He murdered his partner, who had just shot an innocent pregnant woman. His crime was an act against racist police brutality, similar to Mookie's part in burning Sal's Famous, but even more heroic. Bird now works as an investigator for the attorney who has arranged for his parole, Victoria Heller. He also has taken on the job of surrogate father for Jameel, the son of a murdered prison friend. His job during one episode (air day: November 1, 1990) is to help Heller with a sentencing hearing that will determine whether Ernesto Peña, a fifteen-year-old murderer, will spend his life in prison.

Ernesto has watched his idol, basketball player Bobby Jackson, advertise fancy basketball shoes on television. The manufacturer is running a contest: Viewers are supposed to make a videotape of the most memorable, preferably funny, use to which they have put the fancy shoes. Jackson himself will pick the twenty best entries, and the lucky contestants will win $50,000 each. Ernesto doesn't own a home video camera, so he and three friends break into a store and steal one. The director cuts to a *cinema verité* perspective on subsequent action through the lens of the stolen camera. Just after the theft, Ernesto spots someone wearing the shoes Jackson is selling. He and his friends chase their unlucky victim, and just as he is about to get away, Ernesto produces a pistol, shoots him down, and steals his shoes. As Ernesto gloats over his ill-gotten totem, the director pans back from the scene to reveal that the videotape is being played on a monitor in a courtroom. A prosecuting attorney freezes the frame, leaving the picture of Ernesto caught in the act while he finishes his summation for the jury. The jury returns a verdict of guilty on a charge of first-degree murder. The viewer learns that Heller has anticipated a guilty verdict and has planned all along to plead for mercy. She wants the judge to impose a moderate sentence on the grounds that Ernesto is as much a victim as the boy he has murdered.

Bird is at first skeptical about his assignment. He concludes that Ernesto is "a punk killer who deserves to do his time." The boy has not killed for money, or even for a misplaced sense of honor, as a reasonable criminal might; inexplicably, he has killed for a pair of shoes. Bird yields, however, and in due course comes to see that Ernesto has made a naive and bad response to the postmodern condition. He watches videotape of a survey of teenage girls in a shopping mall. They guess that the shoes Ernesto wore on the day of the shooting belong to "a dork, nerd, dweeb"; his stolen shoes, on the other hand, are the fashionable footwear of someone "rich, boss, cool." "I've been out of touch for twenty years," Bird tells Jameel. "I need lessons in cool." In a store at the mall, he learns how costly the shoes are, although they are made of rubber and plastic. He is furious, questioning the salesman's integrity by pointing to a gang of young toughs, "drug pushers," who are the only ones in the neighborhood able to afford the shoes. Bird also discovers most of the conditions thought to be factors mitigating criminal behavior since the days of Clarence Darrow. The boy's mother died when he was six, and his father is a convict. Ernesto has been passed around among several foster homes, but none of his foster parents care enough to come to his trial. Ernesto is without a family, trapped in abject poverty, handicapped by his ethnicity, and one-down in the seemingly all-important adolescent courtship rituals. He has thus become an easy victim of the shoe company's manipulation.

This fragment's judgment of Nike/Jordan/Lee rhetoric is rendered with the fire-and-brimstone subtlety of a raging prophet. Jackson is put on the witness stand, and is forced to confess that his only care was to serve as a model of hope for minority youth. He tearfully swears that he never foresaw such situations arising. "None of us did," says Heller. "We're all to blame." The shoe company's vice president for marketing is confronted with a charge of cynical profiteering, asking $175 for shoes that cost only $19 to make. Heller accuses him of callously targeting a market that has to resort to criminal acts in order to buy his product.

Finally, Ernesto is put on the stand to testify about his own ab-jection. Heller convinces the judge, who shows mercy by sentenc-ing Ernesto to five years of juvenile correction followed by twelve years in prison.

PERORATION:
PUSHING REPRESENTATIONAL POLITICS

The rhetoric of the House Un-American Activities Committee is no longer persuasive. There is no longer a common under-standing of what it means to be and to act as an American. Rare-ly any more do our leaders dream Martin's dream, envisioning a unified, colorblind culture devoted to the principles of social justice. America is now a federation of subcultures—some based on race and ethnicity; others based on gender, age, and sexual orientation. In our new condition, Americans seem to have an insatiable appetite for fragments that represent a vision of who they are, what they hope to accomplish, and how they "fit in" among all the other cultural formations. Some cling to the romance that we will return to "the good old days," that we soon will tire of such intellectual fads as "postmodernism" or "multicul-turalism." Others recognize that there is no going back, but are unable to envision a better response than whining about hyper-real simulations that some of us seem to hold more dear than life's necessities. So, for example, Baudrillard (1989) argues that simulation is probably irreversible. All we can do is promote an iconoclastic art "which does not consist of destroying images, but of manufacturing images, a profusion of images in which there is nothing to see." Mookie shows another way. There is always something to see in simulations. This is true because represent-ations are rhetorical. They are fragmentary exhortations "to be" as "signified." The act of "becoming" fills the emptiest sign with lived humanity. Resistance is possible, even without certain knowledge of our "real" identities, if only because simulations are so profuse. There are as many alternate identifications, even within a single cultural formation, as there are clumps of grass on the veldt. There is therefore a representational politics to be practiced. We cannot act without risk, but we can act in the comfort of realizing that not even elephants walk everywhere all at once, nor will they crush all clumps of grass in their way. The "right thing" may be evident only in such concrete cases as that represented in *Do the Right Thing*. But we can survive the risk of telling, and living, such stories. Furthermore, the capacity to interpret these narratives critically and rhetorically makes "the wrong thing" generally clear. We can even see an imperative: For now, for a moment, for the time being, in the present circumstances, it is right to expose and resist all fetishes that exploit human hunger for a morally active identity. Yo, Michael! Yo, Spike! Look out for the elephant! Stop making Nike commercials! Can you dig it? Can you dig it? Can you dig it?

FURTHER READING

Althusser, L. (1971) *Lenin and philosophy and other essays.* Trans. B. Brewster. New York: Monthly Review Press.

Baudrillard, J. (1981) *For a critique of the political economy of the sign.* Trans. C. Levin. St. Louis, MO: Telos Press.

Baudrillard, J. (1983a) *In the shadow of the silent majorities.* Trans. P. Foss, P. Patton, and J. Johnston. New York: Semiotext(e).

Baudrillard, J. (1983b) *Simulations.* Trans. P. Foss, P. Patton, and P. Beitchman. New York: Semiotext(e).

Baudrillard, J. (1989) Beyond the vanishing point of art. In: P. Taylor, ed., *Post-pop art.* Cambridge, MA: MIT Press, pp. 182–89.

Bitzer, L. F. (1968) The rhetorical situation. *Philosophy and rhetoric, 1,* 1–14.

Bruns, G. L. (1982) *Inventions: Writing, textuality, and understanding in literary history.* New Haven, CT: Yale University Press.

Campbell, J. A. (1990) Between the fragment and the icon: Prospect for a rhetorical house of the middle way. *Western Journal of Speech Communication, 54,* 346–76.

Caplan, H. (1962) A late medieval tractate on preaching. In: A. E. Drummond, ed., *Studies in rhetoric and public speaking in honor of James A. Winans.* New York: Russell & Russell, pp. 51–52.

Chronicle of Higher Education (1990, November 21), pp. A14–A15.

Condit, C. M. (1987) Crafting virtue: The rhetorical construction of public morality. *Quarterly Journal of Speech, 73,* 79–97.

Condit, C. M. (1990) Rhetorical criticism and audiences: The extremes of McGee and Leff. *Western Journal of Speech Communication, 54,* 330–45.

Cox, J. R. (1990) On "interpreting" public discourse in post-modernity. *Western Journal of Speech Communication, 54,* 317–29.

Flatow, S. (1990, December 2) I wanted to be more. *Parade: The Sunday Newspaper Magazine,* pp. 10–13.

Gadamer, H. G. (1976) *Philosophical hermeneutics.* Trans. D. E. Linge. Berkeley: University of California Press.

Gadamer, H. G. (1980) *Dialogue and dialectic: Eight hermeneutical studies on Plato.* Trans. P. C. Smith. New Haven, CT: Yale University Press.

Gadamer, H. G. (1981) *Reason in the age of science.* Trans. F. G. Lawrence. Cambridge, MA: MIT Press.

Gadamer, H. G. (1982) *Truth and method.* Trans. G. Barden and J. Cumming. New York: Crossroad.

Gaonkar, D. P. (1990) Object and method in rhetorical criticism: From Wichelns to Leff and McGee. *Western Journal of Speech Communication, 54,* 290–316.

Gouldner, A. W. (1979) *The future of intellectuals and the rise of the new class.* New York: Seabury Press.

Gramsci, A. (1957) *The modern prince and other writings.* Trans. L. Marks. London: Lawrence & Wishart.

Habermas, J. (1970a) On systematically distorted communication. *Inquiry, 13,* 205–18.

Habermas, J. (1970b) Towards a theory of communicative competence. *Inquiry, 13,* 360–75.

Habermas, J. (1979) *Communication and the evolution of society.* Trans. T. McCarthy. Boston: Beacon Press.

Hirsch, E. D., Jr. (1987) *Cultural literacy: What every American needs to know.* Boston: Houghton Mifflin.

Hirsch, E. D., Jr., J. F. Kett, and J. Trefil (1988) *The dictionary of cultural literacy.* Boston: Houghton Mifflin.

Hyde, M. J. (1983) Rhetorically, man dwells: On the making-known function of discourse. *Communication, 7,* 201–20.

Hyde, M. J., and C. R. Smith (1979) Hermeneutics and rhetoric: A seen but unobserved relationship. *Quarterly Journal of Speech, 65,* 347–63.

Johnstone, H. W. (1970) *The problem of the self.* State College: Pennsylvania State University Press.

Johnstone, H. W. (1990) Foreword. In: R. A. Cherwitz, ed., *Rhetoric and philosophy.* Hillsdale, NJ: Erlbaum, pp. xiv–xix.

Lee, S. (1987) *Inside guerrilla filmmaking.* New York: Simon & Schuster.

Lee, S., with L. Jones (1988) *Uplift the race: The construction of School Daze.* New York: Simon & Schuster.

Lee, S., with L. Jones. (1989) *Do the right thing: A Spike Lee joint.* New York: Simon & Schuster.

Lee, S., with L. Jones, (1990) *Mo' better blues.* New York: Simon & Schuster.

McGee, M. C. (1970) Thematic reduplication in Christian rhetoric. *Quarterly Journal of Speech, 56,* 196–204.

McGee, M. C. (1975) In search of "the people": A rhetorical alternative. *Quarterly Journal of Speech, 61,* 235–49.

McGee, M. C. (1984) Secular humanism: A radical reading of "culture industry" productions. *Critical Studiess in Mass Communications, 1,* 1–33.

McGee, M. C. (1985) 1984: Some issues in the rhetorical study of political communication. In: K. R. Sanders, L. L. Kaid, and D. Nimmo, eds., *Political communication yearbook.* Carbondale: Southern Illinois University Press, pp. 155–82.

McGee, M. C. (1986) Against transcendentalism: Prologue to a functional theory of communicative praxis. In: H. W. Simons and A. A. Aghazarian, eds., *Form, genre, and the study of political discourse.* Columbia: University of South Carolina Press, pp. 108–58.

McGee, M. C. (1990) Text, context, and the fragmentation of contemporary culture. *Western Journal of Speech Communication, 54,* 274–89.

McKerrow, R. E. (1989) Critical rhetoric: Theory and praxis. *Communication Monograph, 56,* 91–111.

Newcomb, H. M., and P. M. Hirsch (1984). Television as a cultural forum: Implications for research. In: W. D. Rowland and B. Watkins, eds., *Interpreting television: Current research perspectives.* Beverly Hills, CA: Sage, pp. 58–73.

Said, E. W. (1983) Opponents, audiences, constituencies, and community. In: W. J. T. Mitchell, ed., *The politics of interpretation.* Chicago: University of Chicago Press.

Schrag, C. O. (1985) Rhetoric resituated at the end of philosophy. *Quarterly Journal of Speech, 71,* 164–74.

Schrag, C. O. (1986) *Communicative praxis and the space of subjectivity.* Bloomington: Indiana University Press.

Schrag, P. (1972, March 25) The failure of political language. *Saturday Review,* pp. 30–31.

Seymour, G. (1990, March 30) Spike and Nike: The making of a sneaky sneaker commercial. *Entertainment Weekly,* pp. 28–33.

Sullivan, A. (1990, July 2) The two faces of Bensonhurst. *The New Republic,* pp. 13–22.

Taylor, C. (1971) Interpretation and the sciences of man. *Review of Metaphysics, 25,* 3–51.

Bibliography of Michael Calvin McGee's Works

Compiled by JOHN LOUIS LUCAITES

Compiler's note: The entries are given in chronological order.

McGee, Michael C. "Thematic Reduplication in Christian Rhetoric." *Quarterly Journal of Speech* 56 (1970): 196–204.

McGee, Michael C. "Edmund Burke's Beautiful Lie: An Exploration of the Relationship between Rhetoric and Social Theory." PhD dissertation, University of Iowa, 1974.

McGee, Michael C. "The Rhetorical Process in Eighteenth Century England." In *Rhetoric: A Tradition in Transition,* ed. Walter R. Fisher. 100–21. East Lansing: Michigan State University Press, 1974.

McGee, Michael C. "In Search of 'The People': A Rhetorical Alternative." *Quarterly Journal of Speech* 61 (1975): 235–49.

McGee, Michael C. "The Fall of Wellington: A Case Study of the Relationship between Theory, Practice and Rhetoric in History." *Quarterly Journal of Speech* 63 (1977): 28–42.

McGee, Michael C. "Prerogative and Tyranny in the Nixon Years." *Exetasis* 4 (1977): 3–12.

McGee, Michael C. " 'Not Men, but Measures': The Origins and Import of an Ideological Principle." *Quarterly Journal of Speech* 64 (1978): 141–55.

190   Bibliography

McGee, Michael C. "The Practical Identity of Thought and Its Expression." In *Rhetoric '78*, ed. Robert Brown and Martin Steinemann. 259–73. Minneapolis: University of Minnesota Center for Advanced Studies in Language, Style, and Literary Theory, 1979.

McGee, Michael Calvin. "The 'Ideograph': A Link between Rhetoric and Ideology." *Quarterly Journal of Speech* 66 (1980): 1–17.

McGee, Michael Calvin. "'Social Movement': Phenomenon or Meaning?" *Central States Speech Journal* 31 (1980): 233–44.

McGee, Michael Calvin. "The Origins of 'Liberty': A Feminization of Power." *Communication Monographs* 47 (1980): 23–45.

McGee, Michael Calvin. "A Materialist's Conception of Rhetoric." In *Explorations in Rhetoric: Studies in Honor of Douglas Ehninger*, ed. Raymie E. McKerrow. 23–48. Glenview, IL: Scott, Foresman, 1982.

McGee, Michael Calvin. "An Essay on the Flip Side of Privacy." In *Argument in Transition: Proceedings of the Third Summer Conference on Argumentation*, ed. David Zarefsky. 105–115. Annandale, VA: Speech Communication Association, 1983.

McGee, Michael Calvin. "Social Movement as Meaning." *Central States Speech Journal* 34 (1983): 74–76.

McGee, Michael Calvin, and Martha Anne Martin. "Public Knowledge and Ideological Argumentation." *Communication Monographs* 50 (1983): 47–65.

McGee, Michael Calvin. "Another Philippic: Notes on the Ideological Turn in Criticism." *Central States Speech Journal* 35 (1984): 43–50.

McGee, Michael Calvin. "Secular Humanism: A Radical Reading of 'Culture Industry' Productions." *Critical Studies in Mass Communication* 1 (1984): 1–33.

McGee, Michael Calvin. "1984: Some Issues in the Study of Political Communication." In *Political Communication Yearbook: 1984*, ed. Keith R. Sanders, Lynda Lee Kaid, and Dan Nimmo. 155–82. Carbondale: Southern Illinois University Press, 1985.

McGee, Michael Calvin. "On Feminized Power." The Van Zelst Lecture in Communication, Northwestern University School of Speech, Evanston, IL, 1985.

McGee, Michael Calvin. "The Moral Problem of *Argumentum per Argumentum*." In *Argument and Social Practice: Proceedings of the Fourth SCA/AFA Conference on Argumentation*, ed. J. Robert Cox. 1–15. Annandale, VA: Speech Communication Association, 1985.

McGee, Michael Calvin. "Recreating a Rhetorical View of Narrative: Adam Smith in Conversation with Quintilian." In *Argument and Social Practice: Proceedings of the Fourth SCA/AFA Conference on Argumentation*, ed. J. Robert Cox. 45–56. Annandale, VA: Speech Communication Association, 1985.

McGee, Michael Calvin, and John S. Nelson. "Narrative Reason in Public Argument." *Journal of Communication* 35 (1985): 139–55.

McGee, Michael Calvin. "Against Transcendentalism: Prologue to a Functional Theory of Communicative Praxis." In *Form, Genre, and the Study of Political Discourse,* ed. Herbert W. Simons and Aram A. Aghazarian. 108–58. Columbia: University of South Carolina Press, 1986.

Scult, Allen, Michael Calvin McGee, and Kenneth Kuntz. "Genesis and Power: An Analysis of the Biblical Story of Creation." *Quarterly Journal of Speech* 72 (1986): 113–31.

McGee, Michael Calvin, and John Lyne. "What Are Nice Folks like You Doing in a Place like This?: Some Entailments of Treating Knowledge Claims Rhetorically." In *The Rhetoric of the Human Sciences: Language and Argument in Scholarship and Public Affairs,* ed. John S. Nelson, Donald McCloskey, and Allan Megill. 381–406. Madison: University of Wisconsin Press, 1987.

McGee, Michael Calvin. "Hide-Bound Argumentation in Discipline-Bound Inquiry." In *Argument and Critical Practices: Proceedings of the Fifth SCA/AFA Conference on Argumentation,* ed. Joseph W. Wenzel. 565–68. Annandale, VA: Speech Communication Association, 1987.

McGee, Michael Calvin. "Power to the 'People.'" *Critical Studies in Mass Communication* 4 (1987): 432–37.

McGee, Michael Calvin. "Rhetoric, Organizational Communication, and Sartre's Theory of Group Praxis." B. Aubrey Fisher Memorial Lecture, University of Utah, 1988.

McGee, Michael Calvin. "A Response to Charles Arthur Willard's *A Theory of Argumentation*." In *Spheres of Argument: Proceedings of the Sixth SCA/AFA Conference on Argumentation,* ed. Bruce E. Gronbeck. 309–13. Annandale, VA: Speech Communication Association, 1989.

McGee, Michael Calvin. "Principles of Liberty: An Argument for Political Rhetorics Rather Than Analytical Philosophies of Freedom." In *The Rhetoric of Liberty in Bozeman, Montana,* ed. Terry L. Anderson and Donald McCloskey. 1–41. Indianapolis, IN: Liberty Fund, 1990.

McGee, Michael C. "Text, Context, and the Fragmentation of Contemporary Culture." *Western Journal of Speech Communication* 54 (1990): 274–89.

McGee, Michael Calvin. "Superficial Confrontations." In *Argument and the Postmodern Challenge: Proceedings of the Eighth SCA/AFA Conference on Argumentaion,* ed. Raymie E. McKerrow. 76–79. Annandale, VA: Speech Communication Association, 1993.

Index